No one else

can match the effectiveness, the simplicity, or the appeal of the

SPECTRUM READING SERIES

Students gain meaningful practice—independently

With the SPECTRUM READING SERIES students not only get the practice they need in essential reading skills, they also enjoy being able to do it on their own.

In grades one through six, each lesson features an illustrated story followed by exercises in comprehension and basic reading skills. Because the same format is used consistently throughout, your students will have little trouble doing the lessons independently. And each two-page lesson can be finished easily in one class period.

Students develop and refine key reading skills.

- **Comprehension** exercises help students go beyond understanding of facts and details to drawing conclusions, predicting outcomes, identifying cause and effect, and developing other higher level comprehension skills.
- **Vocabulary development** builds on words from the reading selections. In addition to learning synonyms, antonyms, and words with multiple meanings, students develop sight vocabulary and learn to use context as a clue for meaning.
- **Decoding** exercises refine students' abilities to "attack" and understand new reading words.
- **Study skills** are developed by helping students apply their reading skills to new tasks, such as using reference materials, reading graphs, and applying other everyday life skills.

Reading selections captivate and motivate.

Students get their best reading practice by actually reading. That's why the selections in the SPECTRUM READING SERIES, in addition to offering practice in skills, also motivate students to read—just for fun.

Students quickly become friends with the characters in these entertaining stories. And they enjoy new levels of reading success—thanks in part to carefully controlled vocabulary and readability as well as beautiful illustrations.

The program adapts completely to any teaching situation.

The SPECTRUM READING SERIES can be used in many different ways.

- For the whole class . . . for intensive reinforcement of reading skills or to supplement a basal reading program.
- For reading groups . . . to provide skills practice at the appropriate levels.
- For individual use . . . to help build a completely individualized program.
- For at-home practice . . . to expand on skills learned in the classroom.

 Children's Publishing

Copyright © 2003 McGraw-Hill Children's Publishing.

Printed in the United States of America. All rights reserved. Except as permitted under the United States Copyright Act, no part of this publication may be reproduced or distributed in any form or by any means, or stored in a database retrieval system, without prior written permission from the publisher.

Send all inquiries to: McGraw-Hill Children's Publishing • 8787 Orion Place • Columbus, Ohio 43240-4027

ISBN 1-57768-464-8

7 8 9 10 11 12 POH 06 05 04 03

The McGraw·Hill Companies

Index of Skills for *Reading Grade 4*

Numerals indicate the exercise pages on which these skills appear.

Knowing the Words

Abbreviations—11, 47, 59, 61, 75
Antonyms—5, 9, 15, 27, 37, 51, 57
Classification—5, 13, 23, 35, 47, 59
Homographs—29, 33, 45, 53, 63, 71
Homophones—19, 39, 65, 79, 83
Idiomatic and figurative language—13, 19, 35, 37, 45, 53, 65, 75, 83
Multiple meanings—7, 17, 25, 41, 49, 55, 69, 77, 85
Sight vocabulary—*All lessons*
Synonyms—3, 11, 21, 31, 43, 61, 67, 73, 79, 81
Word meaning from context—*All activity pages*

Working with Words

Compound words—17, 19, 37, 49, 57, 63, 81, 83, 85
Possessives—13, 15, 33, 35, 51, 53, 55, 59, 61, 75, 77, 79
Prefixes and suffixes—3, 5, 7, 9, 11, 21, 23, 25, 27, 29, 31, 39, 41, 43, 45, 47, 65, 67, 69, 71, 73

Reading and Thinking

Author's purpose—5, 17, 25, 33, 49, 59, 69, 77, 79
Cause and effect—3, 7, 11, 13, 17, 23, 25, 31, 33, 39, 47, 51, 55, 57, 63, 71, 73, 81, 83, 85
Character analysis—5, 15, 23, 35, 39, 53, 63, 73, 81
Comparison and contrast—5, 13, 19, 23, 29, 37, 57, 63, 69, 79
Context clues—9, 15, 21, 27, 35, 43, 49, 53, 57, 61, 65, 71, 75, 77, 79, 83
Drawing conclusions—5, 7, 11, 21, 25, 29, 33, 37, 41, 45, 53, 57, 61, 65, 67, 73, 77, 85
Fact and opinion—9, 19, 25, 35, 47, 51, 59, 67, 85
Facts and details—3, 7, 11, 17, 21, 23, 27, 29, 33, 41, 43, 45, 55, 65, 69, 71, 73, 75, 81, 83
Main idea—3, 9, 15, 19, 23, 27, 31, 39, 43, 47, 49, 51, 55, 59, 63, 67, 71, 75, 81, 85
Predicting outcomes—15, 19, 27, 35, 39, 41, 43, 45, 51, 55, 59, 61, 65, 69, 77, 83
Sequence—13, 21, 31, 41, 49, 53, 61, 67
Summarizing—17, 31, 37, 47, 75, 79, 83

Learning to Study

Alphabetical order—3, 13, 35, 49, 67, 75
Dictionary use— 3, 5, 23, 39, 49, 53, 71, 77, 81
Following directions—*All activity pages*
Charts, graphs, and maps—19, 21, 31, 35, 39, 51, 69, 81, 83
Life-skills materials—17, 27, 37, 57, 61, 63, 73, 85
Outlines—9, 11, 13, 29, 43, 45, 67, 71, 75
Parts of a book—15, 33, 47, 59
Reference materials—7, 23, 25, 41, 55, 63, 65, 73, 79

Editorial Review Board

Joyce Bayless
Principal
Everman, Texas

Patricia A. Bladow
Classroom Teacher
Wales, Wisconsin

Carolyn Clancy
Classroom Teacher
Berkley, Michigan

Carol Colvin
Consultant
Bedford, Texas

Dorothy Cartlidge Cruse
Chapter 1 Reading Teacher
Delhi, Louisiana

MariLouise DeLoughrey
Classroom Teacher
Northport, New York

Toby J. Forden
Resource Specialist
Camarillo, California

Dr. Keith E. Gainey
Former Director of Special
Education
Cleveland, Ohio

Polly K. Galloway
Reading Coordinator
Wilson, North Carolina

Mary O. Gentile
Supervisor of Curriculum
and Instruction
Bensalem, Pennsylvania

Dr. Geraldine H. Jenkins
Director of Kindergarten
and Reading Improvement
East St. Louis, Illinois

Geraldine F. Keenan
Classroom Teacher
Dover, New Hampshire

Norma Kuehnle
Coordinator of Reading and
Language Arts
Rockville, Maryland

Cynthia MacFadden
Language Arts Teacher
Chattanooga, Tennessee

Peggy McCann
Classroom Teacher
Columbus, Ohio

Barbara Morningstar
Classroom Teacher
Fort Lauderdale, Florida

Kayleen Pollard
Classroom Teacher
Cumming, Georgia

Kathryn Ransom
Reading Coordinator
Springfield, Illinois

Betsy F. Reppert
Classroom Teacher
Fredericksburg, Pennsylvania

Carol A. Riley
Director of Curriculum and
Instruction
Medina, Ohio

Yvonne Sayger
Primary Specialist
Merritt Island, Florida

Carol Sullivan
Reading Resource Teacher
Milwaukee, Wisconsin

Nancy J. Wales
Reading Specialist
Hayward, California

Nell Wooten
Classroom Teacher
Marietta, Georgia

SPECTRUM READING
Grade 4

Table of Contents

A Look Back

Read the story to find out the kind of show Ben works on.

1   "This is great! Hurry, Ben, and sit down to watch this tape of last year's show. Your part is almost on," said Robert.

2   Ben was feeling his way into the dark room when he bumped into Ling, the show's producer, who turned and smiled. "Welcome back from vacation, Ben. It's good to see you and the rest of the cast and crew. We just started watching the tape."

3   "Hi, everybody," whispered Ben as he found a place to sit facing the screen in the front of the room. He focused his eyes and saw Cindy and Robert on the screen. They were the hosts on a half-hour children's show called *Just for Openers*. They also did the science parts of the show. Ben started to watch the tape. Robert and Cindy were finishing a report on rain clouds.

4   "Do you recognize that kid?" asked Kim, one of the cast members, as the tape continued.

5   "He sure looks like me," said Ben, laughing. He saw himself up on the screen doing a report for his part of the show, called "Ben, the Traveler." The show was about places and people that children would like to visit.

6   "For this program, Ben was on location. He was in Michigan at a special kind of camp," Ling said. Everyone's attention was back on the screen. Ben was introducing the show: "... *The National Music Camp is a special kind of camp. The campers are artists, dancers, and musicians. They range in age from eight years old to college age. Their days are filled with projects that help them improve their skills in the arts. There is time to practice and learn. There is also time just to play. . . .*"

7   The background tape on the screen changed as Ben continued. The campers were now seen climbing into boats and playing softball.

8   "... *The National Music Camp offers just what these campers want. This is Ben, the traveler, saying good-bye from Michigan.*"

9   "Hold the applause, please!" Ben said.

10   Everyone blinked as the lights came back on. Ling stood and said, "I thought it would help us if we saw a tape of one of last year's shows. Then we can talk about the shows for this year. I'm sure you all have some good ideas to share."

11   "I'm ready to get started," said Ben. "This is going to be the best year ever!"

Knowing the Words

Write the words from the story that have the meanings below.

1. someone in charge of a show _____
   (Par. 2)

2. adjusted to make clearer _____
   (Par. 3)

3. a particular place _____
   (Par. 6)

4. a level of school after high school _____
   (Par. 6)

5. special assignments _____
   (Par. 6)

A **synonym** is a word with the same or nearly the same meaning as another word. Circle each pair of synonyms.

6. location—vacation   8. blink—stare

7. finish—complete   9. bumped—hit

Learning to Study

Number the words in each column in alphabetical order.

1. ____ program   2. ____ interview
   ____ prepare   ____ introduce
   ____ producer   ____ invited

Guide words are printed at the top of most pages in a dictionary. The guide word at the left is the first word on the page. The guide word at the right is the last word on the page. Check each word that could be found on a page having the guide words shown in dark print.

3. **brand—brim**
   ____ brake   ____ broken   ____ break

4. **fast—favor**
   ____ family   ____ father   ____ fame

5. **home—hope**
   ____ host   ____ honest   ____ hotel

Reading and Thinking

Write **T** before the sentences that are true. Write **F** before the sentences that are false.

1. ____ Ben has been on vacation.

2. ____ Ben is a cast member on a program for children.

3. ____ Ben has never worked on the show.

4. ____ Ben does the science reports on the program.

5. ____ Ling is the producer of the show.

6. Check the sentence that best states the main idea of the story.

   ____ Ben tells the cast and crew about his summer vacation.

   ____ Ben shares his ideas for the show with Ling.

   ____ Ben and the cast start a new year working on the show.

7. Why did Ben go to Michigan last year?

   _____

   _____

Working with Words

A **prefix** is a group of letters added to the beginning of a word to change its meaning. The prefix **pre-** means "before." For example, *preview* means "to view before." Add **pre-** to each word below. Use each new word in a sentence.

1. _____ pay _____

   _____

2. _____ heat _____

   _____

3. _____ package _____

   _____

3

Meeting the Cast

How would you feel about being a new cast member?

1 "Before we start discussing ideas for *Just for Openers*, I'd like you to meet Carmen," said Ling. "Carmen is our newest and youngest cast member. I asked her to join us today so she could learn about the program and so she could meet the people she will be working with during the year."

2 The cast gathered around Ling and Carmen. "This is Robert and Cindy," Ling began. "They have been the hosts of the show since it started three years ago. At that time, Robert was just nine years old, and Cindy was ten. Over here is Ben. Ben prepares the travel section of the show. He started with the show at the same time Robert started. Ben and Robert are twelve now."

3 Ling turned and placed her hands on Kim's and Laurie's shoulders. "Laurie and Kim are the other two cast members. This is their second year with the show. They work on other ideas for the show including sports and entertainment," Ling told Carmen. "You saw the cast in action when you watched the tape of last year's show."

4 "I'm glad to meet you," Carmen said, smiling. "I know working on *Just for Openers* will be fun, but I feel pretty nervous right now."

5 "You'll do just fine," said Cindy.

6 "We all felt nervous when we started," said Robert.

7 "I still get nervous when the show starts a new year," Ben said, "and then I relax and just have fun."

8 "Kim and I understand how you feel, Carmen," said Laurie, "because we were new to the show last year. All of us help each other, and Ling and the crew work hard to make sure everything fits together."

9 Just then the door opened. Everyone turned and watched. Two adults walked into the room. "Carmen, I'd like you to meet the film crew members," said Ling. "James and Nancy tape and record the shows outside the studio. The crew often travels out of the city to tape sections for the show in other places."

10 James and Nancy smiled at Carmen. "I'm glad we'll be working with you, Carmen," said James.

11 "Since you've all been so nice, I can stop being nervous and start having fun," Carmen said, smiling.

Knowing the Words

Write the words from the story that have the meanings below.

1. talking about _____
   (Par. 1)

2. part _____
   (Par 2)

3. counting each piece
   as a part of the total _____
   (Par. 3)

4. rest _____
   (Par. 7)

In each row, circle the three words that belong together.

5. cast   crew   topics   producer

6. travel   parents   sports   science

7. city   camera   film   photography

8. speak   discuss   talk   turn

A word that means the opposite of another word is an **antonym**. Find an antonym in the story for each of the words below.

9. finish _____
   (Par. 1)

10. scattered _____
    (Par. 2)

11. calm _____
    (Par. 6)

12. apart _____
    (Par. 8)

Learning to Study

Circle the words in each column that would fit between the guide words.

1. **chew—cotton**
   child
   certain
   comedy

2. **refresh—rush**
   regain
   raise
   rim

3. **handle—huddle**
   hamper
   hang
   huge

4. **tape—transport**
   tardy
   tax
   trespass

Reading and Thinking

Write **C** before the groups of words that describe Carmen and **B** before the groups of words that describe Ben.

1. _____ youngest of the cast members

2. _____ worked on the show for three years

3. _____ knows most of the cast members

4. _____ has no experience on this show

5. _____ works on a travel section

6. The groups of words below describe a character in the story. Write the character's name in the blank.

   oldest cast member   host of show

   _____

7. Check the reason the author probably wrote this story.

   _____ to give facts about Ben's trip

   _____ to give facts about the cast

   _____ to give facts about Carmen

8. How do you know that Carmen felt better after talking to the cast and crew?

   _____

   _____

Working with Words

The prefix **mis-** means "badly." For example, *misbehave* means "to behave badly." Add **mis-** to each word. Then write the meaning of the new word.

1. _____ spell _____

2. _____ match _____

3. _____ place _____

4. _____ read _____

5. _____ judge _____

Good Ideas

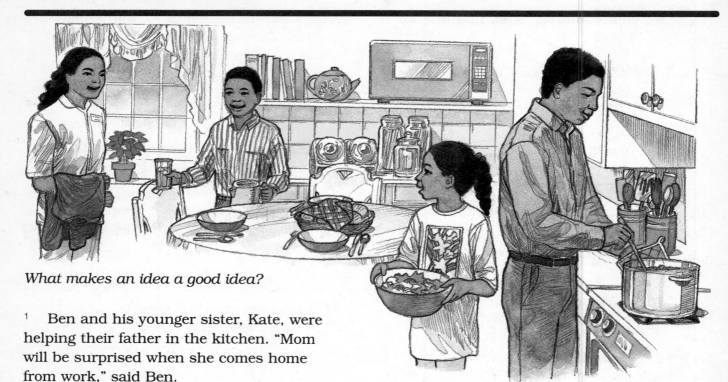

What makes an idea a good idea?

1   Ben and his younger sister, Kate, were helping their father in the kitchen. "Mom will be surprised when she comes home from work," said Ben.

2   "This was a great idea," said Ben's dad.

3   Soon they heard the slamming of a car door. Kate turned to her left and raced to the back door. She saw her mother, in her nurse's uniform, walking toward the house. "Welcome home, Mom," Ben said.

4   Kate exploded with the news. "We fixed dinner! It wasn't even hard to do."

5   "What a wonderful surprise," said Mrs. Wilkins. "Whose idea was this?"

6   "We all thought of it," said Mr. Wilkins.

7   "I'm certainly glad you did," she said as she hugged her family and sat down at the table. Dad, Kate, and Ben continued fixing dinner as Mom sipped her iced tea.

8   "Speaking of good ideas, how was your meeting for *Just for Openers?*" asked Mom.

9   "I'm really excited about the program this year. Ling was happy with many of our suggestions," Ben answered.

10   Kate stopped stirring the chili. "Did you use my ideas about going to Disney World and the Baseball Hall of Fame?" she asked.

11   "Yes, I did. No one was surprised that the idea about the Hall of Fame was yours. Ling said that she thinks you enjoy baseball more than anyone in Chicago," Ben said, faking a throw to Kate.

12   "Dinner is ready," announced Dad.

13   Everyone joined Mom at the table. "I've saved the best news for last," said Ben, smiling. "I talked to Ling about going to Washington, D.C., to tape information for my first show. She thought it was a great idea. She's making plans for us to go before school starts. You're all invited to come along."

14   "I'll have to miss this trip, Ben. I don't think I should take time off right now. But Kate will be able to go since she is still on summer vacation," said Mom.

15   "Yes, and my school calendar is about the same as yours, so I'll be able to go with you and Kate," Dad said.

16   "Good ideas do run in this family," said Mom. "Now how about some more of that delicious chili?"

Knowing the Words

Write the words from the story that have the meanings below.

1. took a small drink _____
   (Par. 7)

2. ideas or hints _____
   (Par. 9)

3. pretending _____
   (Par. 11)

Check the meaning of the underlined word in each sentence.

4. Mom was <u>fixing</u> the lamp when the telephone rang.
   ____ repairing
   ____ preparing

5. My friend and I wanted to <u>run</u> for the same class office.
   ____ move quicker than walking
   ____ be in an election

6. I <u>left</u> the stage after my speech.
   ____ opposite of "right"
   ____ went away

7. Kate had a <u>hard</u> time making the chili.
   ____ solid
   ____ difficult

Learning to Study

Write the number of the encyclopedia volume that would have the most information for each of these topics.

Vol. 1	Vol. 2	Vol. 3	Vol. 4	Vol. 5	Vol. 6	Vol. 7
A–C	D–F	G–J	K–M	N–Q	R–T	U–Z

1. ____ presidents
2. ____ horses
3. ____ baseball
4. ____ eagle
5. ____ whales
6. ____ bikes
7. ____ nurses
8. ____ cooking

Reading and Thinking

Write **T** before the sentences that are true. Write **F** before the sentences that are false.

1. ____ Ben's mom is a nurse.
2. ____ Kate had the idea to fix dinner.
3. ____ Ben's mom asked about his meeting.
4. ____ It was Ben's idea to go to the Baseball Hall of Fame.
5. ____ The whole family will go to Washington, D.C.
6. ____ Ling thought the trip should be planned at a later time.

7. Ben's dad could go with his children to Washington, D.C., because _____

   _____.

   _____

8. Why wasn't Ling surprised by Kate's idea about the Baseball Hall of Fame?

   _____

   _____

9. How do you think Ben's mom feels about the family trip to Washington, D.C.?

   _____

   _____

Working with Words

The prefix **non-** means "not." For example, *nonmetal* means "not metal." Add **non-** to each word below. Then write the meaning of the new word.

1. _____ profit _____

2. _____ stop _____

3. _____ electric _____

A Home for the President

Would you like to be President and live in the White House?

1   Ben stood outside the black wrought-iron gate and stared because he couldn't believe he was standing where he was. It was Kate, tugging on his shirt, who brought back his attention.

2   "What a terrific place! I wish I could be President and live in there!" said Ben.

3   "You never know, Ben," Mr. Wilkins said as he winked at Kate. "This could be your address in the future."

4   "If you were living here now," said Kate, "you'd be getting company. That's what I wanted to show you, Ben. Look at the cars with the tiny flags on the hoods."

5   As they watched, a long black car pulled up to the gate closest to them. A guard had a brief talk with the driver of the car. Then the gate swung open, and the car drove up to the White House. More vehicles came, each with a flag from a different country.

6   "Dad," Kate whispered, "what's going on?"

7   "I think those cars are bringing guests from other countries to have dinner at the White House," said Mr. Wilkins.

8   "I'm glad we don't have to wash the dishes," sighed Kate.

9   Dad and Ben looked at each other and chuckled. Each of them continued to watch the parade of cars.

10   "You know," said Dad, "what you're seeing isn't the original White House."

11   "It's a fake?" asked Kate.

12   "Well, not exactly. During a war in 1814 the British burned the White House. A rainstorm put the fire out, but only the outside walls were left. The inside had to be completely rebuilt. Then, one hundred years after the rebuilding of the inside, the walls began to crack from old age. Experts thought the White House was ready to cave in," explained Dad.

13   "It looks fine to me," said Ben.

14   "That's because workers hollowed out the White House in 1948 and constructed stronger walls. The inside was built to look just as it had looked before. The President had to live someplace else for the four years it took to finish the project."

15   "I know one thing," said Ben. "If I were President, I'd make sure the work was finished so I could live in the White House."

Knowing the Words

Write the words from the story that have the meanings below.

1. wonderful _____
   (Par. 2)

2. forms of transportation _____
   (Par. 5)

3. first _____
   (Par. 10)

4. emptied on the inside _____
   (Par. 14)

5. made _____
   (Par. 14)

A word that means the opposite of another word is an **antonym.** Find an antonym in the story for each of the words below.

6. past _____
   (Par. 3)

7. long _____
   (Par. 5)

8. removing _____
   (Par. 7)

9. real _____
   (Par. 11)

Learning to Study

An **outline** is used to put ideas in order. It can be used to show important facts from a story. Use the facts from paragraph 12 to complete Part I. Then use the facts in paragraph 14 to complete Part II.

I. The White House is damaged and rebuilt
   A. Fire began by the British in 1814
   B. Rainstorm puts the fire out
   C. Inside is completely rebuilt
   D. _____
   E. _____

II. The White House is rebuilt again
   A. Walls are made stronger
   B. _____
   C. _____

Reading and Thinking

Circle the word that best completes each sentence.

1. The _____ is trained to give information to a tour group.

   worker   guide   tourist

2. Ben had to complete the _____ for his show before the deadline.

   path   company   project

3. Check the sentence that best states the main idea of the story.
   _____ The Wilkins family watches cars arrive at the White House.
   _____ Ben sees and learns about the White House before the tour.
   _____ One President didn't live in the White House.

A **fact** is something that is known to be true. An **opinion** is what a person believes. It may or may not be true. Write **F** before the sentences that are facts. Write **O** before the sentences that are opinions.

4. _____ People from many countries visit the White House.

5. _____ Everyone would like to live in the White House.

6. _____ The first White House was burned in 1814.

7. _____ The British should have rebuilt the White House after it burned.

Working with Words

Think of the meaning of the prefix in each word. Then write the meaning of the word.

1. misshape _____

2. presale _____

3. nonliving _____

9

A Special Change

Would you be excited to see a history maker?

1   As their tour bus traveled through Arlington National Cemetery, Ling told Ben, "I can't believe our good luck with your first show."

2   "You must mean the weather," Ben teased. Ling was always looking at the sky when the outdoor parts of the show were being taped.

3   Ling playfully tugged the brim of Ben's cap over his eyes. "You know what I mean," Ling said. "The White House tour was great and now we get to tape a history maker. The first female honor guard will take part in today's Changing of the Guard."

4   The tour bus came to a stop and Ben, Kate, their father, and Ling walked to the steps facing the Tomb of the Unknowns. The film crew followed.

5   Mr. Wilkins whispered to Kate, "No one knows the names of the soldiers buried in the tomb. It is guarded day and night to honor all Unknown United States soldiers who died in battle."

6   They all watched the pacing guard walking back and forth in front of the tomb. He walked the same number of steps in each direction. The guard turned at exactly the same place every time. He tapped his heels together with each turn.

7   The crowd stood as the Changing of the Guard was announced. An officer appeared. He inspected the uniform and rifle of the new guard. With a loud tap of her heels, Sergeant Heather Lynn Johnsen began pacing in the same way as the first guard. The officer and the first guard then marched away. The ceremony had ended. The guards hadn't spoken a word.

8   "How did she get to be a part of the honor guard?" Kate rushed to ask Ling.

9   "The same way as any of the soldiers who guard the Unknowns," Ling said. "She went through the same training that all the honor guards did. I read that she received a perfect score on her exam."

10   "Training and exams?" Ben said. "What does an honor guard need to be able to do?"

11   Ling replied, "Besides being able to march, the guard members must know the cemetery history. They must be able to give the exact location of nearly two hundred burial plots."

12   "Working on my questions for the show is enough for me," Ben joked. "I'd better start thinking about tomorrow's taping at the Washington Monument."

 Photograph by Reuters / Luc Novovitch / Archive Photos

Knowing the Words

Write the words from the story that have the meanings below.

1. a place for burying _____
   (Par. 4)

2. walking back and forth _____
   (Par. 6)

3. looked at closely _____
   (Par. 7)

4. a special service _____
   (Par. 7)

5. a test _____
   (Par. 9)

Abbreviations are shortened forms of words. Match the word in the first column with its abbreviation.

6. ___ United States   **a.** Mr.

7. ___ Mister   **b.** D.C.

8. ___ District of Columbia   **c.** U.S.

A **synonym** is a word with the same or nearly the same meaning as another word. Circle each pair of synonyms.

9. guarded—protected **12.** hurry—rush

10. tugged—pulled   **13.** sit—stood

11. whispered—shouted **14.** piece—part

Learning to Study

Use the facts from paragraph 7 to complete Part I. Then use paragraph 11 to complete Part II.

I. Changing of the Guard
   A. Officer inspects rifle and uniform

   B. _____

   C. _____

II. Guard Training
   A. Do precise marching

   B. _____

   C. _____

Reading and Thinking

1. What did Ling, Ben, Mr. Wilkins, and Kate see at Arlington National Cemetery?

   _____

2. When is the Tomb of the Unknowns guarded?

   _____

3. Why is the Tomb of the Unknowns guarded?

   _____

   _____

4. Why is Sergeant Johnsen a history maker?

   _____

5. How do you think Ben felt about the job of becoming an honor guard?

   _____

Working with Words

The prefixes **im-** and **in-** mean "not." For example, *impatient* means "not patient." *Inactive* means "not active." The prefix **im-** is usually used before words that begin with *b*, *m*, or *p*. The prefix **in-** is usually used before words that begin with other letters. Add **im-** or **in-** to each word below. Use each new word in a sentence.

1. _____ possible _____

   _____

2. _____ experience _____

   _____

3. _____ balance _____

   _____

World Underground

Would you like to tour a cave?

1   Mr. Wilkins never thought his family would get so excited about his idea. At lunch five days ago, he had talked about going to Mammoth Cave. Now they were there.

2   "Let's go in with the next group," said Mr. Wilkins. "I've never been inside a cave before. I'm ready to take the tour."

3   Once the group was inside the cave, the guide began the tour. "In the early days of this nation, folks came on horseback and by stagecoach to see Mammoth Cave. During the War of 1812, an ore used in making gunpowder was prepared in these caves and shipped out by wagon train," said the guide.

4   The group moved on. Pam, the guide's assistant, continued the tour. "As soon as your eyes get used to the dim light, you'll see stone icicles. These dripstones look like spears. They grow down from the ceiling and up from the floor. They are formed by water dripping from the ceiling. The water carries bits of limestone with it. As the water drips, limestone builds up forming the dripstones," she told them.

5   Both Ben and Kate reached out to touch one of the stone icicles. Before their fingers were close to the dripstones, they heard Pam's warning. "Be careful not to touch any," she said. "The oil from your fingers can keep the wet limestone from sticking to itself. Then the dripstones will stop growing."

6   Later the tour group was asking about the Echo River that flows through part of the cave. "It is at the lowest level of the cave," the guide said. "The river is three hundred sixty feet below ground."

7   As Mrs. Wilkins listened to the guide, she remembered to ask about the fish she had heard about. "What kind of fish swim in caves?" she asked Pam.

8   "Some are Kentucky blindfish. They live in total darkness and have no eyes," Pam explained. "The fish can feel movement in the water and changes in water pressure. That helps the blindfish know where they are. It also helps them find food."

9   "The cave tour has been fun," Ben said. "The stone icicles were my favorite things in the cave."

10   "You can have more fun and learn more about caves by joining a caving club," said Pam.

11   "Let's join!" exclaimed Kate.

Knowing the Words

Write the words from the story that have the meanings below.

1. the overhead part of a room _____
   (Par. 4)
2. a type of rock _____
   (Par. 4)
3. a force or weight _____
   (Par. 8)

In each row, circle the words that belong together.

4. listening   noticing   looking   ceiling
5. club   ore   rocks   limestone
6. helper   assistant   guide   level

7. A **simile** is a figure of speech. It compares two things using *like* or *as*. For example, *the sunshine felt like fire* is a simile. Write the simile used in paragraph 4.

   _____

Learning to Study

1. Complete the outline below. Use the facts from paragraph 3 to complete Part I. Use the facts from paragraph 4 to complete Part II.

   I. Early days of Mammoth Cave
      A. Visitors came on horseback and by stagecoach

      B. _____

   II. How dripstones are formed

      A. _____

      B. _____

Number the words in each column in alphabetical order.

2. ____ lantern   3. ____ million
   ____ locate   ____ midnight
   ____ lane   ____ mention

Reading and Thinking

1. Number the events to show the order in which they happened.

   ____ Pam described blindfish.

   ____ The guide told the tour group that folks came to Mammoth Cave by stagecoach.

   ____ Mr. Wilkins suggested a trip to Mammoth Cave.

   ____ The tour group learned about the Echo River.

   ____ Pam gave a warning.

2. You shouldn't touch dripstones because

   _____.

3. The fish in Mammoth Cave are called

   blindfish because _____.

Write **E** before the sentences that tell about the early days of Mammoth Cave. Write **N** before the sentences that tell about Mammoth Cave now.

4. ____ The cave is open for tours.
5. ____ Ore used in gunpowder is prepared.
6. ____ A tour includes a look at dripstones.
7. ____ People ride horses to the cave.

Working with Words

Add **'s** to singular nouns to show a person or thing owns something. Make the noun after each sentence possessive. Then write that form in the sentence.

1. The _____ tour through the cave was interesting. (family)

2. Pam knew the _____ rules. (club)

3. The _____ stories made the tour interesting. (guide)

A Narrow Escape

Can you learn from a scary experience?

1 Ben, his family, and Pam were climbing the stairs leading out of Mammoth Cave. "How do you know so much about caves?" Ben asked Pam.

2 "I was born in New Mexico, near Carlsbad Caverns. Caving is popular there and here in Kentucky. My entire family belongs to a caving club. We explore caves as often as we can," she answered. "You have to like dark, narrow tunnels and mud if you want to enjoy caving."

3 "Mud likes me," said Kate. "That makes me a natural in caves."

4 Ben and Pam just laughed. "Don't you worry about getting lost or stuck in caves?" Ben asked.

5 "I don't worry about that now, but I remember when I did. The first time I went into a cave, I was about your age, Kate," said Pam. "Everything was fine during the first part of the exploring. Then suddenly I couldn't move. My parents had gone through a very narrow passage. Now I was stuck in the same passage. As I yelled and started to panic, my parents turned around and rushed to my rescue. When Dad reached me, he bent down to the ground by my feet. Then he stood up, gave me a hug, and told me to follow him through the passage."

6 "Were you able to do it?" asked Ben.

7 "I certainly could. I thought it was some kind of a magic trick. Once we joined Mom, my dad told me that this experience should teach me to remember two important things. I should always remember to wear my safety equipment, and I should always remember to tie my shoes," Pam said, smiling. "I really wasn't stuck at all. My shoelace had been caught under a rock."

8 "I bet you learned to check your shoes after that," said Ben, laughing.

9 "That's not all I learned. I joined a caving club soon after my first time in a cave. Since then, I've learned about caves and caving safety by being a club member. An adult caver always comes with us. No one ever goes into a cave alone. We always tell someone where we're going and when we expect to be back," explained Pam. "The club wants the members to be safe while they're having fun."

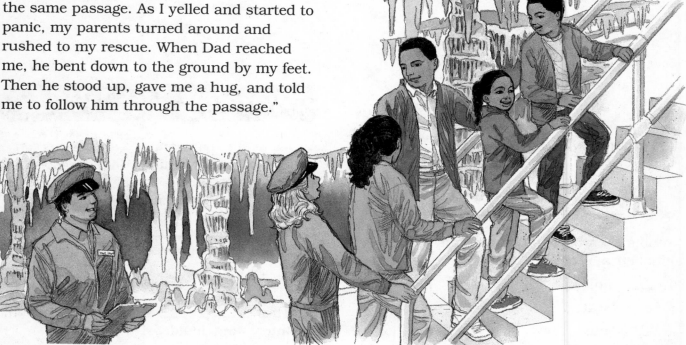

Knowing the Words

Write the words from the story that have the meanings below.

1. opening _____
   (Par. 5)

2. have great fear _____
   (Par. 5)

3. necessary supplies _____
   (Par. 7)

A word that means the opposite of another word is an **antonym.** Write the pair of antonyms from each sentence.

4. The lantern's bright beam helped us to see through the dark passage of the cave.

   _____

5. My friends often explore caves, but they seldom go without some club members.

   _____

Learning to Study

A **table of contents** is on one of the first pages in a book. It shows the chapters that are in the book. It also shows the page each chapter begins on. Use the table of contents below to answer the questions.

Adventures Underground
Table of Contents

1. How many chapters are in the book?

   _____

2. Write the title of the chapter that may tell about finding Mammoth Cave.

   _____

3. On what page does "Cave Beauty" begin?

   _____

Reading and Thinking

Circle the word that best completes each sentence.

1. Because she liked caves, it was ____ for Pam to be the guide's assistant.

   popular   natural   necessary

2. The guide was ____ the cave tour.

   talking   pointing   leading

3. Check the sentence that best states the main idea of the story.
   ____ Pam discusses caving.
   ____ Cavers should tie their shoes.
   ____ Caving alone is dangerous.

4. Will Pam stay a caving club member?

   Why or why not? _____

   _____

5. What makes Pam good at guiding people through caves?

   _____

Working with Words

Add an apostrophe to the end of a plural noun that ends in **s** to show that a person or thing owns something. For example, the bones of the dogs would be written as *the dogs' bones.* Make the plural noun after each sentence possessive. Then use the possessive form of the word in the sentence.

1. We can still enjoy the _____ discoveries. (Native Americans)

2. The _____ equipment fills a van. (explorers)

3. Some _____ habits are odd. (bats)

4. The _____ supplies were checked. (members)

Riders in the Wind

Why do you think someone would join a bicycle club?

1 Ling decided to do her biking earlier than usual one morning. Riding her bike was one of her favorite hobbies. She rode the bike trails in the park close to her apartment. She dressed quickly and started pedaling to the park. There were several different trails. She had tried and enjoyed each one of them.

2 She wasn't alone on the trails. She waved to several people she knew. The ride had been good exercise, and she was on her way home when she felt something was wrong with her bike. It got harder and harder to pedal. Ling came to a stop and inspected her bike. She had been right. Her front tire was flat.

3 Ling was close enough to her apartment to walk the rest of the way. As she walked

by the corner, just before the entrance to her street, she saw the newspaper stand. As usual, she stopped and bought a paper.

4 A photograph on the front page of the newspaper caught her attention. The picture was of a large group of people, of all ages, riding bicycles. The sentences under the picture explained. A bicycle club was riding through the city. They would be staying in town overnight. Ling opened the newspaper. She found the article on the page listed under the picture. Ling began to read:

5 Soldier Field will be home for more than fifty bike riders today. They will stay tonight and then leave to finish their eight hundred mile trip.

6 The club, called the Pedalers, was formed three years ago by Mike and Rose Glenn. They like to ride bikes, and they like people. They joined the two and formed a bike club.

7 The club takes short day trips each weekend of the year. There are also longer trips to interesting places. These trips take hours of planning. The bikers must work hard to build their strength for the long trips. They must be able to ride eighty to one hundred miles a day.

8 Members often sleep in strange places during these trips. Mrs. Glenn said the oddest place the Pedalers have stayed was in a lighthouse.

9 The club members like to meet people when they stay in a city. The public is invited to talk with members of the club while they are in town.

10 Ling closed the paper and tucked it under her arm. As she walked her bike back home, she decided to spend some time talking to the members of the Pedalers.

Knowing the Words

Write the words from the story that have the meanings below.

1. pushing with your feet _____
   (Par. 1)

2. opening to something _____
   (Par. 3)

3. picture from a camera _____
   (Par. 4)

Check the meaning of the underlined word in each sentence.

4. The items for the sale were on a <u>stand</u> at the end of the counter.
   _____ be on your feet
   _____ table

5. Ann wore a costume to the party given by our <u>club</u>.
   _____ a large stick
   _____ a special group

Learning to Study

A newspaper **index** lists many sections that have information you may need or want. Write the number for the sections you would use to find the information listed below.

INDEX

Advertisements	G6–14
Business	E1–19
Entertainment	D1–12
City	B1–7
Sports	B8–17

1. last night's game score _____

2. movie times _____

3. mayor's meetings _____

4. paper route job _____

5. name of new factory manager _____

6. closed city streets _____

Reading and Thinking

Write **T** before the sentences that are true. Write **F** before the sentences that are false.

1. _____ Ling likes to ride her bike.

2. _____ Ling belongs to the Pedalers.

3. _____ Ling heard from a friend that the bike club was in town.

4. What must bikers do to ride long trips?

   _____

5. Check the reason the author probably wrote this story.
   _____ to tell about a special club
   _____ to tell about Ling's flat tire
   _____ to tell about bike trails

6. A **summary** is a short sentence that tells about a topic. To make a summary you must find the most important facts. The sentence below is a summary for paragraph 6.

   The Glenns formed a bicycle club.

   Underline the sentence below that is the best summary for paragraph 7.

   Bikers work hard to build strength.

   The bike club takes long and short trips.

Working with Words

A **compound word** is a word made by combining two smaller words. Write the two words that make up the underlined compound word in each sentence.

1. I asked two friends to stay <u>overnight</u> after we worked at the school play.

   _____

2. Our class wrote a school <u>newspaper</u>.

   _____

Wheels

Have bikes always been the way they are today?

1   Ling was working very hard at the studio when the phone rang. "Hi, Ben," she said. "What a nice surprise to hear from you." As she listened to Ben, Ling began to smile.

2   "I read the same article in the newspaper about the bike club," said Ling. "I plan to talk with the club members tonight. You're welcome to meet me there, and I can take you home when we're finished." After Ben checked with his mom, he made plans to meet Ling that night.

3   Ling had met many people by the time Ben arrived. She was having fun talking with the bike club members. Ben joined Ling while she was having a conversation with a club member.

4   "Ben, this is Ann Marsh. We've been talking about the history of bikes," said Ling. "Ann likes to read books about the invention and history of the bicycle, just as I do."

5   "The only thing I know about bikes is that I like to ride them," Ben said. He looked around. Then he pointed at the bikes propped against the walls. "My bike looks like some of these," he said.

6   "Bikes look very different today than they looked in the past," said Ling.

7   Ann agreed. She began telling Ben some of the history of the bicycle. She told him the first bike was invented in France in 1790. It looked like a wooden horse on wooden wheels. The first bike was called a walk-along. The rider made it go by pushing with his or her feet. There was no way to steer it until nearly thirty years later. Then the horse's head was replaced by a handle. That allowed the rider to turn the front wheel. In 1839, a blacksmith added foot pedals that turned the back wheel.

8   The most well-known of the early bikes was the high-wheeler. This bike had a large front wheel and a small rear wheel. The rider sat over the front wheel. It was about five feet high. The rider had to take a running leap just to get on the seat.

9   The bicycle of today appeared in 1890. Both wheels were the same size and the bikes used pedal brakes. This kind of bike has been ridden ever since then.

10   After listening Ben said, "It sounds as if the only thing that hasn't changed about bicycles is the fun we have riding them."

Knowing the Words

Write the words from the story that have the meanings below.

1. talk between two or more people _____
(Par. 3)

2. leaned _____
(Par. 5)

A word that sounds the same as another word but has a different spelling and meaning is a **homophone.** Draw a line under the homophone that correctly completes each sentence.

3. The _____ was still on the grass when Ling left to ride her bike. (dew, do)

4. The _____ a bike looks has changed over the years. (way, weigh)

5. Write the sentence from paragraph 7 that has a simile. _____

_____

Learning to Study

A **bar graph** is used to compare different things. This bar graph shows total distances traveled every year by the club. Answer the questions using the graph.

1. In what year did the club travel over three thousand miles? _____

2. In what year did the club travel the least? _____

Reading and Thinking

1. Check the sentence that best states the main idea of the story.

____ Riding a bicycle is fun.

____ Bikes have changed over the years.

____ Ling introduces a new friend.

2. Will bikes change in the future? Why or why not? _____

_____

Write **M** before the words that could describe modern bicycles. Write **E** before words that could describe some of the early bicycles.

3. ____ is pushed with the feet

4. ____ has seat five feet off the ground

5. ____ uses brakes

6. ____ has wooden wheels

Write **F** before the sentences that are facts. Write **O** before the sentences that are opinions.

7. ____ Bike riding is the best exercise.

8. ____ Everyone enjoys riding a bike.

9. ____ The first bike was invented over one hundred years ago.

10. ____ All bikes should look the same.

Working with Words

Use two words from each sentence to make a compound word. Write the compound word in the blank.

1. The rain was so heavy during the storm, some streets were flooded.

_____

2. The cables that are under the ground need to be fixed.

_____

Niagara Falls

Read this story to learn about Niagara Falls.

1 "I didn't know there are two Niagara Falls," Ben said, shouting. His dad could hardly hear him over the roar of the Falls. Cindy and Robert were with them. They stood on a platform high above the water. The mist from the Falls made rainbows in the sun.

2 "The Falls near us is the American Falls," Ben's dad yelled back. "The Falls on the Canadian side is much bigger. It is called Horseshoe Falls because of its shape."

3 Ben, Robert, and Cindy had flown in from Chicago with Mr. Wilkins that morning. They were going to tape science and travel sections for the show on location at Niagara Falls. They would meet Ling and the studio crew later in the afternoon.

4 Cindy shouted, "It's hard to believe that all this water from both Falls is just *part* of the water that could be here."

5 "There's more water than this?" Robert asked, surprised. "Where is it?"

6 "I read that before the water gets to the Falls, part of it is sent into four huge tunnels," Cindy told him. "The tunnels lead to power plants. These plants use the force of the water to make electric power."

7 "What if the plants use too much water? The Falls will become a trickle!" said Ben.

8 "That won't happen," Cindy said. "The power plants can take only a certain amount of water. That way there will be plenty of water. The Falls will stay as beautiful as they are now."

9 "Who uses all that power?" asked Ben.

10 "People do," his dad answered. "Electricity is made from the power of the Falls. It is used to light homes and run machines."

11 Later, they met Ling and the crew, and they all went to see the Cave of the Winds together. They put on yellow raincoats and walked behind the Falls. They stood behind a roaring curtain of water as James and Nancy started to tape. James and Nancy began to look upset. They worked harder to keep the spray off of the equipment than they did to tape the show. It was so loud that Cindy and Robert's report couldn't be heard over the noise. They just smiled and waved at the camera. Soon the crew stopped taping to protect the camera from the mist.

12 "I should have gotten a raincoat for the equipment," said James. "I never thought the water would be such a problem. This is the first time both the camera and I got soaking wet on a sunny day."

 Photograph by Phil Degginger / Tony Stone Images

Knowing the Words

Write the words from the story that have the meanings below.

1. a raised flat stand _____
    (Par. 1)

2. small amount of
    running liquid _____
    (Par. 7)

3. kind of power _____
    (Par. 10)

A **synonym** is a word with the same or nearly the same meaning as another word. Write the pair of synonyms from each sentence.

4. The force of the falling water was used to make the power for the city.

    _____

5. He yelled directions to the girl as she shouted over the loud noise.

    _____

Learning to Study

Read the chart. Write **T** before the sentences that are true. Write **F** before the sentences that are false.

Niagara Falls Tourist Information			
	Number of Tourists		
States	1992	1994	1996
Maine	18,751	16,402	19,576
Ohio	35,783	37,914	43,587
Georgia	27,982	25,431	28,587

1. _____ In 1992 most tourists came from Georgia.

2. _____ More people from Maine came to the Falls in 1996 than in 1992.

3. _____ Each year the fewest number of tourists came from Maine.

4. _____ The number of tourists from Georgia was larger each year.

Reading and Thinking

1. Number the sentences to show the order in which things happened.

    _____ Ben met Ling and the studio crew.

    _____ Ben arrived at Niagara Falls.

    _____ The crew stopped taping.

    _____ The cast and crew toured the Cave of the Winds.

    _____ Sections of the show were taped.

Circle the word that correctly completes each sentence.

2. A friend's opinion about an idea can _____ the way we think about that idea.

    meet   shape   believe

3. Cindy was _____ that Ling knew to meet her at the gate.

    confused   upset   certain

4. Where does this story take place?

    _____

5. What kind of power is made by using the water from the Falls?

    _____

6. Will Cindy and Robert need to give their reports on Niagara Falls again? Why or

    why not? _____

    _____

Working with Words

Underline the prefix in each word. Then write the meaning of the word.

1. inaction _____

2. preview _____

3. misjudge _____

21

Lucky Boy

What could happen if a person was pulled over Niagara Falls?

1   "Welcome to the *Maid of the Mist*. I'm the captain on the Niagara Falls tour boat. I hope nobody here is worried about getting wet," he said, laughing. He steered the boat toward the Falls.

2   This was the second day at Niagara Falls for Ben, his dad, and the crew. This time James decided not to take any chances. He didn't want the water to ruin the taping. "Let's start taping before the boat gets too close to the Falls. I don't want the mist attacking the camera again," he said to Nancy.

3   "We've seen quite a few wet people on this boat," the captain was saying with a smile. "The *Maid* has been sailing in these waters since 1846."

4   "Have you ever had any problems?" asked Ben as he adjusted his life jacket.

5   "We've had very few problems," said the captain. "However, a few years back we did rescue a boy who was in real trouble. It seems that he was boating with some friends on the river above the Falls. The boat sank, and the water took the boy over the Falls. He was only seven years old!"

6   The people in the boat stared at the captain, waiting for him to finish his tale.

7   "What happened?" Ben asked finally.

8   "Oh, he just got some scratches and bruises. He was lucky! Other people have died going over the Falls," the captain said. He went back to steering the boat. His listeners looked at each other, wondering if the captain's story was true.

9   "That's a true story," Mr. Wilkins told Ben and his friends. "It happened in 1960. The crew of this boat rescued the boy from the water."

10   Ben looked at the Falls roaring down so close to the boat. He could feel the force of the water pounding the rocks, and the noise was deafening. It was hard to believe a boy could live through such a dangerous fall.

11   Later, when the boat moved away from the Falls, Cindy and the crew taped a science section for the show. "The Falls have two kinds of rocks under them," Cindy began. "The rock on top is tough and wears away slowly. The rushing water has left a ledge of hard rock that lets the water fall with tremendous force."

12   As Ben listened, he kept picturing the young boy being pulled over the Falls. The captain had been right. That boy was lucky!

Knowing the Words

Write the words from the story that have the meanings below.

1. made changes _____
(Par. 4)

2. saved _____
(Par. 9)

3. so loud you cannot hear _____
(Par. 10)

4. very large _____
(Par. 11)

In each row, circle the words that belong together.

5. rescued   wet   saved   preserved

6. mist   spray   rock   water

7. believe   drive   steer   handle

8. problem   trouble   chance   difficulty

9. stared   listened   looked   noticed

Learning to Study

1. Under what main topic in an encyclopedia could you find facts about both of these things?

   Maid of the Mist   Horseshoe Falls

   _____

2. What letter would you look under to find the volume with the best facts about the

   main topic you chose? _____

The first word in dark print in each dictionary entry is the entry word. An entry word can have more than one meaning. Read the dictionary entry below. Then write the number of the meaning used in each of the sentences that follows.

   roar /rōr/ *n* 1 the deep cry of a wild
      animal 2 a loud continuing sound

3. ____ We heard the roar of the water before we could see the Falls.

4. ____ The lion's roar surprised us.

Reading and Thinking

1. Check the sentence that best states the main idea of the story.

   ____ The cast learns about a rescue.

   ____ Ben knows life jackets can save your life.

   ____ Being a captain on the *Maid of the Mist* takes training.

2. When did the *Maid of the Mist* begin

   sailing at the Falls? _____

3. The boy went over the Falls because ____

   _____.

4. The rock under the Falls wears away

   because _____

   _____.

5. Check the words that describe the captain.

   ____ honest   ____ shy

   ____ friendly   ____ trained

6. How was the boy's experience described by the captain different from the experience of others who went over

   the Falls? _____

   _____

Working with Words

A suffix is a group of letters added to the end of a base word to change its meaning. The suffix -ous can mean "has much." For example, *famous* means "has much fame." Add -ous to each word. Then write the meaning of the new word.

1. joy____   _____

2. humor____ _____

Up, Up, and Away!

How do you think it would feel to ride in a hot air balloon?

1   Ben and Kim were sitting in the meeting room at the TV studio. They were with Ling and the other cast members. "You rode in a hot air balloon?" Ben asked Kim.

2   "I couldn't wait to tell you!" Kim said with a big grin. "While some of you went to Niagara Falls, my family and I visited my Aunt Kelly in New Mexico. Aunt Kelly has a hot air balloon. She flies it in the Albuquerque International Hot Air Balloon Fiesta. While I was there, Aunt Kelly took me for a ride!"

3   "Was it scary?" asked Robert.

4   Kim smiled. "At first I was scared," she admitted. "When we were first in the air, I felt as if I had left my stomach back on the ground. Then I began to relax. Aunt Kelly knows just how to handle her balloon. She has flown it for more than five years with no problems. I had a great time."

5   Ben said, "I don't understand how hot air balloons work. Why do they have a heater that hangs underneath the balloon?"

6   "I didn't know the answer to that question either until my aunt explained how important heat is to ballooning. The heater warms the air inside the balloon," Kim explained. "Warm air rises, so the balloon goes up. When the air cools off, the balloon descends. That's why the pilot keeps turning the heater on and off."

7   "How do pilots steer the balloons in the direction they want to go?" Carmen asked.

8   Kim smiled and said, "You can't steer the balloon! You just go where the wind blows you. During the fiesta they have a contest. You drop a marker from a balloon on a certain spot miles away from the starting point to win. Sometimes no one comes close. The wind can blow all of the balloons away from the spot!"

9   "How often does the balloon fiesta take place?" Ling asked.

10   "They've held one each October since 1972," Kim said. "The first year there were only sixteen balloons. This year my aunt said there were five hundred balloons. Thousands of people from around the world attend the festival. Some of the people come to race, but most of the people come to watch the hundreds of balloons fill the sky."

11   Ben smiled as Ling suggested that he and Kim go to the fiesta next year to tape a travel show. "I can see it now. Kim and I are floating high in the New Mexico sky. Look out, birds. Here we come!" said Ben.

Photograph by John D. Pearce

Knowing the Words

Write the words from the story that have the meanings below.

1. below something _____
   (Par. 5)

2. comes down _____
   (Par. 6)

3. are present _____
   (Par. 10)

Check the meaning of the underlined word in each sentence.

4. Since the owner knew how to <u>handle</u> a hot air balloon, Kim felt safe when she took her ride.

   _____ something used to control

   _____ able to take care of something

5. The girls were <u>admitted</u> to the show after they bought their tickets.

   _____ say you know or feel something

   _____ allowed to enter

6. Kim asked her aunt if she could <u>watch</u> the race from the air.

   _____ something that keeps time

   _____ see

Learning to Study

An encyclopedia contains facts about many topics. Facts about the same main topic may be listed under different words. Kim wants to know more about other kinds of air transportation. Write three topics that she could use to find the facts she wants. Do not write *hot air balloons* as one of your topics.

1. _____

2. _____

3. _____

Reading and Thinking

Write **F** before the sentences that are facts. Write **O** before the sentences that are opinions.

1. _____ People race hot air balloons.

2. _____ No one likes to ride in a hot air balloon.

3. _____ Hot air balloons can't be steered.

4. _____ More people attend the festival now than when it started.

5. _____ If you own a hot air balloon, you would like the balloon fiesta.

6. Check the reason the author probably wrote this story.

   _____ to give the history of the hot air balloon

   _____ to tell about hot air ballooning

   _____ to tell about New Mexico

7. What happens when the heater under the basket warms the air inside the

   balloon? _____

8. Write a sentence the author used to make you think Ben and Kim might fly

   in a hot air balloon. _____

   _____

Working with Words

The suffix **-ment** can mean "the act of." For example, *announcement* means "the act of announcing." Add **-ment** to the base words. Then write the meaning of the new word.

1. enjoy _____ _____

2. agree _____ _____

3. measure _____ _____

4. arrange _____ _____

Toy in the Sky

What kind of work would you do on an island?

1   "I'm trying to imagine it," Ben whispered.

2   "Imagine what?" Ling asked.

3   "The days of the Nantucket whalers," Ben replied.

4   Ben, Ling, and Ben's father, Mr. Wilkins, were riding the ferry to Nantucket Island. The trip gave Ben plenty of time to think. "How did the sailors feel about their work? Were they afraid or excited as they hunted the whales?" he wondered aloud.

5   "It sounds as if you have some questions ready for today's story," Ling said. "The guide at the Whaling Museum can answer them. The museum's collection will make you think of even more questions, if I know you," she teased.

6   Ben had been looking forward to this trip ever since he saw the show's schedule. Ling had told him that Nantucket was full of interesting stories. Ben quizzed her about one of these stories.

7   "Ling, who was it that made your last trip here so special?" he asked.

8   "You must be talking about the Kiteman," Ling smiled as she spoke. "We went straight to his house for our story. We were greeted out front by a friendly man wearing a derby hat."

9   "Hello. I'm Al Hartig. Most people know me as the Kiteman of Nantucket," he said.

"Let's go out back and fly some kites as we talk."

10   Ling went on, "The crew started filming as Mr. Hartig taught me how to get one of his kites into the air. Soon I felt I was ready to pilot the kite toward the sky. The kite started upward and then dipped. I gave the string a tug. The brightly colored triangle went toward the sky just as the Kiteman said it would."

11   "As I flew the kite, Mr. Hartig told me about his kites," Ling said. "He told me that each kite is different from any other kite because it is made by hand. More than twenty-five thousand Nantucket Kiteman kites had been made that way."

12   "What a job!" Ben exclaimed. "Ling, do you think Nantucket has always been a home to people with unusual jobs?"

13   "You could say that," Ling answered. "You could also say it draws people who are looking for an adventure."

14   Ben grinned, "That describes me, all right. I hope the cameras are ready for my adventure today."

Knowing the Words

Write the words from the story that have the meanings below.

1. boat that carries people or cargo across water _____
   (Par. 4)

2. hat with a rounded shape _____
   (Par. 8)

3. figure with three sides _____
   (Par. 10)

A word that means the opposite of another word is an **antonym.** Find an antonym in the story for each of the words below.

4. shouted _____
   (Par. 1)

5. brave _____
   (Par. 4)

6. downward _____
   (Par. 10)

7. ordinary _____
   (Par. 12)

8. frowned _____
   (Par. 14)

Learning to Study

Read the directions below and answer the questions.

Drive through town going south and turn left at the first stoplight. Go straight for seven blocks and turn right at the service station on the corner. If you pass the library, you missed the turn. I live in the second to the last house on the right.

1. In what direction do you need to go to get to the first stoplight?

   _____

2. What would you pass if you've missed the turn? _____

3. Is the house on the right or left side of the street? _____

Reading and Thinking

Circle the word that correctly completes each sentence.

1. Every week the restaurant has a ____ dinner prepared for a lower price.

   plate   special   burnt

2. I gave the rusty door a strong ____.

   yell   stare   tug

3. Check the sentence that best states the main idea of the story.

   ____ Nantucket is a famous island.

   ____ Nantucket has a lot to discover.

   ____ Nantucket has a whaling museum.

4. Where can Ben get his whaling questions answered?

   _____

5. What was the Kiteman's real name?

   _____

6. Why are all of the Kiteman's kites different? _____

7. What do you think Ben will discover in Nantucket? _____

Working with Words

The suffix **-less** can mean "to be without." For example, *worthless* means "to be without worth." Add **-less** to each base word below. Use each new word in a sentence.

1. smoke _____ _____

   _____

2. care _____ _____

   _____

27

Whale Watch

Are whales more like fish or people?

1   Ben stood with his dad and Ling at the rail of a sightseeing boat. He was searching for whales in the ocean off Cape Cod. The crew from Nantucket was with them on the boat, taping the whale watch scene for "Ben, the Traveler."

2   Ben was just enjoying the boat ride when he heard his dad asking him a question. "Didn't you study whales in school, Ben?"

3   "Yes, Dad. I didn't think learning about whales would be interesting. I really thought they were oversized fish," said Ben, "but I was wrong. Whales aren't fish at all. They're more like people because they breathe through lungs, not gills. The air goes in and out through a blowhole on top of their heads. A whale also has skin like a person instead of scales like a fish."

4   The boat captain was listening and said, "You learned a lot about whales. The whales we'll see out here today will be humpbacks. They have little knobs on their heads and long, knobby flippers. Years ago, before the whales were protected from hunters, we hardly ever saw humpbacks. They swam so close to shore that the hunters could easily kill them. Since a law started protecting them in 1966, we see more humpbacks

every year," continued the captain. "Now we just watch them and appreciate their special beauty."

5   Ben listened to the captain. He kept looking out over the water. "What's that?" asked Ben. He pointed off to the right of the boat. The crew turned their camera in the direction he was pointing. "It looks like steam or something!"

6   "Good for you! You've spotted a humpback!" shouted the captain. "That 'steam' is warm air from its blowhole hitting the cooler air out here."

7   As they watched, an immense fifty-ton whale, longer than the boat, rolled over in the waves and slapped the water with its extra long flippers. Ben laughed as spray flew high in all directions.

8   "Wow!" Ben said. He turned to face the crew's camera and wiped salt water off his face. "I think that whale has what it takes to make a big splash on television."

Knowing the Words

Write the words from the story that have the meanings below.

1. covering of a fish _____
(Par. 3)

2. bumps _____
(Par. 4)

3. to be grateful _____
(Par. 4)

4. very large _____
(Par. 7)

A word that is spelled the same as another word but has a completely different meaning is a **homograph.** For each pair of meanings below, write one of the homographs that is listed.

      point   scales   kind

5. a. nice
   b. a type of something

   _____

6. a. to show using a finger
   b. the tip

   _____

7. a. instruments used for weighing
   b. covering of a fish

   _____

Learning to Study

Complete the following outline. Use paragraph 3 to complete Part I. Use paragraph 4 to complete Part II.

I. Humpback whales are like people

  A. _____

  B. _____

II. Humpbacks needed protection

  A. _____

  B. _____

Reading and Thinking

Write **T** before the sentences that are true. Write **F** before the sentences that are false.

1. ____ Whales use their lungs to breathe.

2. ____ Whales needed protection.

3. ____ Whales are large fish.

4. ____ Humpback whales have smooth heads.

5. Why did Ben change his opinion about studying whales? _____

_____

6. Why are there more humpback whales today than there were before 1966?

_____

_____

Write **B** before the facts Ben knew about the whales before he talked to the captain. Write **A** before the facts Ben knew after he talked to the captain.

7. ____ The heads of humpbacks have knobs.

8. ____ Whales aren't fish.

9. ____ Whales have skin.

10. ____ A law was passed in 1966 to protect humpback whales.

Working with Words

The suffix **-able** means "capable of." For example, *affordable* is "capable of being afforded." Add **-able** to each word below. Use each new word in a sentence.

1. punish _____ _____

_____

2. defend _____ _____

_____

Freedom Trail

Did you ever want to visit the past?

1 "I'm really tired tonight, Dad. I'm going to write in my journal for a while and then get some sleep," said Ben.

2 "You may be too tired to write tonight. Don't forget, we're leaving early in the morning to go back home to Chicago," reminded his dad.

3 "I'll see how long I can stay awake. See you in the morning, Dad," said Ben as he crawled into bed, yawning. He opened his notebook and began to write.

4 What a trip! Nantucket was great, and the whale watch was exciting. But today my feet hurt and I'm worn out. Doing my travel show is fun, but it can really make me tired. I never thought we'd finish walking Boston's Freedom Trail today. One and a half miles didn't *sound* long, but the message never got to my feet.

5 Our guide was great. He has been a guide for five years. He told me why this job as a guide on the Freedom Trail was perfect for him. He said his name was Ben, like mine, and he lived on Franklin Lane. At first I didn't understand. Then I started to laugh. He was putting Ben and Franklin together for Ben Franklin. Franklin was an important historical figure. I thought the guide's reason was funny.

6 When you walk the Freedom Trail, you pass some of Boston's most famous historical landmarks. As usual, I had my favorites. The first was the Old South Meeting House. Our guide told us the Boston Tea Party was planned there in 1773. Some colonists were to dump the British cargo into the harbor. I could almost hear the plans being made.

7 I liked seeing the Old North Church, too. Our guide said that during the time of Paul Revere, lanterns were hung at the church. The lanterns warned the colonists of an attack by the British. I remembered reading about the lanterns and the ride of Paul Revere in my history book.

8 Walking the Freedom Trail was fun. It was like walking through a period of history. My feet still hurt, but I'm glad I had an opportunity to visit a part of the past. Good night.

9 Ben put down his pen and read what he had written. Even though he was tired, it had been a good day. He closed his notebook, turned out the light, and fell asleep.

Knowing the Words

Write the words from the story that have the meanings below.

1. personal book of writing _____
   (Par. 1)

2. well-known places _____
   (Par. 6)

3. people who live in the colonies _____
   (Par. 6)

4. chance _____
   (Par. 8)

A **synonym** is a word with the same or nearly the same meaning as another word. Write the words from the story that are synonyms for these words.

5. drop _____
   (Par. 6)

6. goods _____
   (Par. 6)

7. evening _____
   (Par. 8)

Learning to Study

Reading maps makes it easier to find your way. Read a map Ben could use as he walks the Freedom Trail. Then answer the questions.

1. If Ben walks west from the statue of Benjamin Franklin, what is the next

   building he'll see? _____

2. In what direction should you walk to go from the State House to the Old West

   Church? _____

Reading and Thinking

1. Number the events to show the order in which they happened.

   ____ Ben wrote in his journal.

   ____ Ben walked the Freedom Trail.

   ____ Ben traveled back to Chicago.

   ____ Ben said he was tired.

   ____ Ben fell asleep after a long day.

2. Check the sentence that best states the main idea of the story.

   ____ Ben doesn't like to walk.

   ____ Paul Revere is important in history.

   ____ Ben learns about Boston's history.

3. The lanterns were hung in the Old

   North Church because _____

   _____

   _____.

4. A summary includes important facts about a topic. The sentence below is a summary for paragraph 6.

   Boston has many historical landmarks.

   Underline the sentence below that is the best summary for paragraph 7.

   Paul Revere's ride is in the history books.

   Lanterns at a church warned the colonists of an attack.

Working with Words

Underline the suffix in each word. Then write the meaning of the word.

1. payable _____

2. mountainous _____

3. priceless _____

4. acceptable _____

Night Light

How can a lighthouse save lives?

1 "You went to Boston?" Laurie asked Ben. They sat in the meeting room at the TV studio, waiting for Ling and the other cast members. "Did you see any lighthouses?"

2 "I did see one from the plane just before we landed," Ben replied. "It was on a small island out in Boston Harbor."

3 "That's Boston Light!" Laurie told him. "Ever since I lived in Maine, I've been interested in lighthouses. There seems to be a story about each one."

4 Ben asked, "What kind of story do you know about Boston Light?"

5 "An interesting one," Laurie told him. "Boston's seaport has always been busy. It needed a signal light to warn ships about the dangers in its harbor. Boston Light was the first lighthouse in America. It was built in 1716. The first Boston Light was made of wood."

6 "It doesn't sound very sturdy," Ben remarked.

7 "You're right. Most of the first lighthouses had to be rebuilt many times. Some were destroyed by storms. Others burned when the fire for the signal light got out of control," Laurie told Ben.

8 "They built fires in the lighthouses?"

9 Laurie answered Ben's question. "At first all they had were wood and coal fires, candles, and oil lamps. Lenses and metal reflectors made the candles and oil lamps seem brighter than they were," Laurie told Ben. "It was two hundred years before lighthouses had electric lights."

10 "Were all the ships safely guided into the harbor by Boston Light?" Ben asked.

11 "No, they weren't," Laurie said, shaking her head. "Some ships still crashed on the rocks. Lighthouses can't do anything about how a ship is handled in rough and stormy seas. Some lighthouse keepers had to row out to the wrecks and save the sailors. One time the Boston Light keeper and his helpers saved twenty-four men from a shipwreck."

12 "Do keepers still save people?" Ben asked.

13 "Well, lighthouses have changed. Many of them are run by computer so no one lives in them. The newest lighthouses also look different from the old-fashioned ones. They are made of steel and look like radio towers," Laurie told Ben.

14 When they heard voices in the hallway, Ben said, "I think Ling and the others are coming now. When Ling gets here, let's ask her if we could do a show on lighthouses."

15 Laurie beamed. "What a bright idea!"

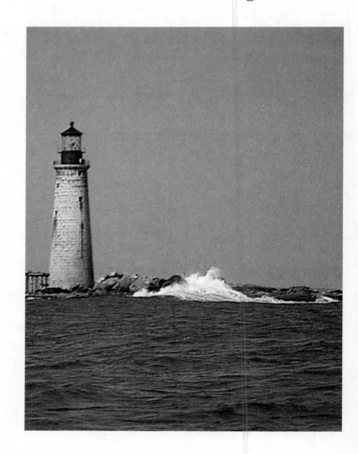

Knowing the Words

Write the words from the story that have the meanings below.

1. strong _____
   (Par. 6)

2. something that
   sends back light _____
   (Par. 9)

3. not modern _____
   (Par. 13)

Check the meaning of the underlined homograph as it is used in the sentence.

4. The sales clerk returned my change.

   ____ money from a larger amount

   ____ make different from what is

5. I learned to cast the fishing line by watching my friend.

   ____ people who act in a show

   ____ throw

Learning to Study

Use the table of contents below to answer the questions

Early Lighthouses

1. What is the title of the first chapter?

   _____

2. What chapter would tell how lighthouses look? _____

3. What pages could you read to find out about the lighthouse Ben saw? _____

4. On what pages would you find facts about safety problems in lighthouses?

   _____

Reading and Thinking

Write **T** before the sentences that are true. Write **F** before the sentences that are false.

1. ____ Boston Light was built in 1716.

2. ____ No lighthouses have been destroyed by fire.

3. ____ Coal fires were used in lighthouses.

4. ____ Lighthouses always saved ships.

5. ____ Some lighthouses use computers.

6. Do you think many lighthouses have been destroyed by fire in the last fifty

   years? Why or why not?_____

   _____

7. Even with modern lighthouses, ships

   may still wreck because _____

   _____.

8. Check the reason the author probably wrote this story.

   ____ to tell about sea rescues

   ____ to give facts about lighthouses

   ____ to give facts about Maine

Working with Words

Fill in each blank with the possessive form of the word in parentheses.

1. We learned the _____ history. (seaport)

2. The _____ purpose was to warn ships of dangers. (lighthouse)

3. The _____ wreck may not have happened if the captain had followed the lighthouse beam. (ship)

4. The _____ program keeps the lighthouse working. (computer)

Lost and Found

Have you ever lost something you really needed?

1   "Ben, why are you searching through your closet? I thought you had a report to do for school," said Ben's mom.

2   "The report for school is why I've got my head stuck in the closet," Ben replied. "I'm looking for some information I found on a place called Old Sturbridge Village. It's a historical village Dad and I heard about when we went to New England. It sounded like a neat place, but we ran out of time to go there. I was stuck for a topic to use for my class report, and then I thought of that place. I just wish I could find that paper."

3   Just then Kate walked into Ben's room. She was blowing a large bubble from a wad of gum, which popped all over her face. Ben turned and saw Kate in the room as she was peeling the gum from her face. Kate bent over to get something from the floor to wrap her gum in when Ben yelled at her.

4   "Stop shouting, big brother," complained Kate as she put her hands over her ears.

5   "That's just what I've been looking for," said Ben, grabbing for the paper, "so give it to me."

6   "You want my bubble gum?" asked Kate.

7   "What I want is in your hand," said Ben. "I've been looking for that paper. I must have thrown it out by mistake. Thanks, Kate," said Ben, smiling. "Now take a hike so I can do this report."

8   "I was a superhero just a few seconds ago. Oh, well! Good luck with the report."

9   Leaving a mess on the floor by his closet, Ben sat down at his desk and read the information. Old Sturbridge Village was the idea of two brothers. They wanted to make a place where people could live and work just as they had two hundred years earlier. "That was long before cars and computers," thought Ben.

10   Ben read that sheep are raised in the village. When the sheep are sheared, the wool is made into yarn. The wool yarn may be dyed with the juice from wild berries or roots. The yarn is then knitted into mittens, scarves, and sweaters. Visitors to Old Sturbridge can watch these events from start to finish.

11   Ben paused and looked toward his closet. He thought about the work that would have gone into each piece of clothing in early America. "I'd still like to visit Old Sturbridge," he thought, "but I'm glad I don't have to live and work there."

Knowing the Words

Write the words from the story that have the meanings below.

1. confused heap _____
   (Par. 9)

2. to have clipped wool _____
   (Par. 10)

In each row, circle the words that belong together.

3. college   school   university   report

4. kitchen   village   hall   lobby

5. searching   seeking   looking   sleeping

6. An **idiom** is a group of words that has a special meaning. For example, *to give someone a hand* means "to help someone." Write the idiom found in paragraph 7 that has the meaning below.

   go away _____

Learning to Study

Number the words in each column in alphabetical order.

1. ____ machine   2. ____ velvet
   ____ melt   ____ vase
   ____ match   ____ valley

Read a map of a historical village to answer the questions.

3. What building do you go through to enter the village? _____

4. What two shops are closest to the exit?

   _____

Reading and Thinking

Circle the word that best completes each sentence.

1. The man ____ about the broken lamp.

   regained   complained   realized

2. Ben had to keep his ____ when he stood on the beam.

   balance   report   exit

3. Check the words that describe Kate.

   ____ helpful   ____ selfish
   ____ shy   ____ funny

Write **F** before the sentences that are facts. Write **O** before the sentences that are opinions.

4. ____ Sturbridge Village is a historical village.

5. ____ It would be fun to live in a historical village.

6. ____ It was harder to do things in the 1700s than it is to do things now.

7. ____ Sturbridge Village is in New England.

8. Do you think Ben will change his room so he can more easily find what he

   needs? Why or why not? _____

   _____

Working with Words

Fill in the blank with the possessive form of the word in parentheses.

1. Ben read about the _____ experiences. (visitors)

2. The _____ owners were dressed in costumes. (stores)

3. The _____ ideas were used to make the village. (brothers)

Slip and Slide

Is learning something new always easy?

1 "I'm really glad you and your family could come with us," Cindy said. "You're going to like skiing."

2 "I hope you're right, Cindy. I'm not sure about this whole idea. Is it hard to learn to ski?" Ben asked anxiously.

3 Cindy smiled at her friend and said, "Don't worry, Ben. The instructor in the beginners' ski class will get you and your family started."

4 Cindy and her parents headed to the chairlift that would take them up to the slopes. Ben's parents went to the adult ski class, while Ben and Kate started in the young beginners' group. Everyone planned to meet in the lodge later in the day.

5 To Ben's surprise, the first thing the children's class practiced was falling

backward with their skis on. "I can already do that!" Kate said proudly. In an instant she was sprawled on her back in the snow, and then she attempted to stand up. "Help!" Kate shouted, as she found herself in a tangle of ski equipment.

6 Mary, their instructor, chuckled as she looked down at Kate. "You'll get up by taking one step at a time. First, lie on your back and hold your skis up in the air."

7 Kate plopped back down and stuck her feet straight up. Her skis wobbled as she awkwardly attempted to hold them still in the air. Snow fell from her skis and hit her in the face. "Hurry, or I'll become a human snowball," laughed Kate, wiping her face.

8 "You're doing fine," said Mary. "Now put your skis down as close to you as you can, side by side, and get up."

9 Struggling a little longer, Kate got back on her feet and asked with a grin, "Am I a ski expert yet?"

10 "You did a terrific job, Kate," said Ben as he brushed snow from the back of Kate's jacket. "It looks as if we're heading to the beginners' slope."

11 As they glided to the slope, Ben heard his name. He turned and saw his parents waving at them. His mom and dad were holding on to each other and laughing as they tried to get up the small slope— sideways.

12 Ben turned back to his own class. He couldn't believe his eyes. Kate was skiing down the beginners' slope! "This is great. Wait until you try it, Ben," shouted Kate as she glided past her brother.

13 Just then Ben's ski tips crossed, and he landed facedown in the snow. "I won't have to worry about trying out for the ski team," sighed Ben.

Knowing the Words

Write the words from the story that have the meanings below.

1. spread out awkwardly _____
   (Par. 5)

2. tried _____
   (Par. 5)

3. twist into a mess _____
   (Par. 5)

4. moved smoothly _____
   (Par. 11)

A word that means the opposite of another word is an **antonym.** Write the pair of antonyms from each sentence.

5. Kate steadied her skis, but then they wobbled and she began to fall.

   _____

6. Kate slipped backward on the slope when she tried to move forward.

   _____

7. What do you think the words *couldn't believe his eyes* mean in paragraph 12?

   _____

Working with Words

Form a compound word by writing one of the words from the list in each blank.

line   base   flake

1. snow _____

2. _____ ball

3. side _____

Use each compound word from above in a sentence.

4. _____

5. _____

6. _____

Reading and Thinking

Write **K** before phrases about Kate. Write **B** before phrases about Ben.

1. ____ enjoys skiing

2. ____ thinks skiing might be hard

3. ____ learns to get up after falling

4. ____ skis down beginners' slope

5. ____ falls over crossed skis

6. Write a sentence from the story that tells you Kate skied before Ben.

   _____

   _____

7. Underline the sentence below that is the best summary for paragraph 5.

   Ben was surprised to see Kate fall.

   Kate fell and couldn't get up.

Learning to Study

Use the information on the poster to answer the questions.

All-Day Rentals	
Boots	$ 9.10
Skis	$13.00
Poles	$ 5.00
All equipment	$15.00
(Boots, Skis, Pole)	

1. Can Ben rent all the equipment he needs for skiing? _____

2. How much would it cost to rent skis?

   _____

3. How long can you use the equipment you rent? _____

4. What equipment has the lowest rental cost? _____

Determined Skier

Why is Cindy's friend such a special skier?

1 Ben was sitting in the snow at the bottom of the beginners' slope when Cindy first saw him in the morning. He had been making a last attempt to ski before his family and Cindy's left for home. His skis were tangled together, and his clothes were covered with snow. "You don't look very happy," said Cindy. "What's wrong?"

2 "I guess I'm just not meant to be a skier," Ben said sadly. "I give up."

3 "You need some words of encouragement, and I know just the person to give them to you," Cindy said kindly. She shaded her eyes against the sun as she searched a slope high up the mountain. Soon Cindy began waving her arms as a figure dressed in blue raced down the mountain toward them. "This is perfect timing because I see her now."

4 Ben watched Cindy's friend skiing at top speed. As he watched, he thought that no one else had to work as hard as he did to learn to ski. Suddenly, he saw that the skier had only one ski. He was going to say something to Cindy about that when he realized something else. Cindy's friend had only one leg.

5 The skier he had been watching skied up to join them. "Pat," Cindy said as her friend came to a complete stop, "I'd like you to meet Ben. This is his first time skiing. He could use some advice and some words of encouragement."

6 "Ben," Pat began, "skiing is something like riding a bicycle because the key is in your balance. I'll take the chairlift up to the slope. Then I'll ski down slowly, and Cindy can tell you what I'm trying to do. Maybe that will help, and then you can try again."

7 After Pat headed toward the chairlift, Ben found his voice. "How does she do that?" he asked Cindy.

8 "Pat is a champion skier. She practices very hard all winter long. She told me this year she will try out for the U.S. Disabled Ski Team," Cindy told Ben.

9 "Do other people with disabilities ski?" asked Ben.

10 "Pat told me that last year more than four hundred skiers entered the Disabled National Championships. Some ski with one leg. Others ski with two artificial legs," Cindy said as Ben watched Pat ski down the slope.

11 Cindy started to tell Ben what Pat was doing as Pat slowly skied down the slope. Ben began to follow her advice. The tips of his skis crossed, and he fell again. This time he just smiled. "The best lesson Pat gave me today is to keep trying," Ben said. "I know I can do that."

Knowing the Words

Write the words from the story that have the meanings below.

1. giving hope _____
   (Par. 3)

2. helpful suggestion _____
   (Par. 5)

Draw a line to match each homophone with its meaning.

3. close   food from an animal
4. clothes   the opposite of *yes*
5. know   to shut
6. no   things worn on the body
7. meet   to have certain information
8. meat   to join

Learning to Study

Entry words are divided into syllables to show where the words can be divided at the end of a line of writing. Write these words in syllables.

1. bottom _____

2. tangle _____

3. mountain _____

The graph shows how much snow fell three days before Ben went skiing. Read the graph. Then answer the questions.

Snowfall

Wednesday :
Thursday :
Friday :
Inches: 0   2   4   6   8

4. What day had the most snowfall?

   _____

5. What is the largest snowfall, in inches,

   recorded on the graph? _____

Reading and Thinking

1. Check the sentence that best states the main idea of the story.

   _____ Cindy introduces a friend.

   _____ Determined people can succeed.

   _____ Skiing takes balance and practice.

2. Cindy introduces Pat to Ben because

   _____.

3. Pat practices so hard because _____

   _____

   _____.

4. What do you think Ben will do after watching and talking to Cindy's friend?

   _____

5. Circle the words that describe Pat.

   strong   lazy   helpful   friendly

Working with Words

Check the correct meaning of the underlined word.

1. Cindy knew Ben needed <u>encouragement</u> when she found him in the snow.

   _____ act of encouraging

   _____ not encouraging

   _____ full of courage

2. The ski slopes are in a <u>mountainous</u> area.

   _____ not a mountain

   _____ full of mountains

   _____ small mountains

3. He thought learning to ski was <u>hopeless</u>.

   _____ without hope

   _____ having hope

   _____ giving hope

Helping Hands

Will machines ever replace people?

1 Kate always looked forward to Saturday mornings because she didn't have to get up as early as she did on school days. She could take her time eating breakfast. Even her mom and dad weren't rushed on Saturdays. Kate thought Saturday was the best day of the week except for one thing. Saturdays meant cleaning her room.

2 "Wake up, sleepyhead," said Ben, shaking Kate. "You'll sleep the day away."

3 "I don't want to get up," said Kate. "I have a terrific idea," she mumbled. "You get started cleaning our rooms, and I'll get up when you're finished."

4 "No way," said Ben, pulling Kate out of bed. "We'll eat first, and then we can work."

5 After breakfast, Ben and Kate went to their rooms. Kate picked up a dirty pair of sneakers from the floor and tossed them into the bedroom closet saying, "I need a robot."

6 Ben heard her. He started to chuckle and asked, "What would you do with a robot?"

7 "I'd make it do things for me," answered Kate. "I saw a movie in school yesterday, and it showed how robots make work safer and easier. If they can do that, they can pick up sneakers!"

8 "I wouldn't know about training a robot to do your chores, but I do know they can do certain types of work. What kinds of things did they do?" Ben asked as he tossed a pillow at Kate.

9 Kate explained, "The movie showed how robots can be useful in dangerous places. They can explore the ocean floor. They can be used to paint bridges and wash windows on tall buildings."

10 "All right, robots make those jobs safer. How do robots make work easier?" Ben quizzed her.

11 "I'll tell you," said Kate. "The robots act like strong arms and hands. They can sort packages and deliver office mail. Some robots load and unload things. Other robots can even package goods in factories. Neatest of all are robots that can be used like fingers and hands. A disabled person's voice tells a special kind of robot to lift and move things. The robot can even make a phone call."

12 "Wow! How does each robot know what to do?" asked Ben.

13 "The guy in the movie explained that these robots are run by computers. The steps of a job are stored in the robot's memory. When the computer gives a command," Kate told Ben, "the robot follows those steps."

14 "Listening to you makes it sound as if robots are just as good as working people," said Ben. "Can I replace you with a robot?"

15 "There's a big difference between people and robots," Kate replied. "Robots can't think, and they don't make good sisters!"

Photograph by John Madere / The Stock Market

Knowing the Words

Write the words from the story that have the meanings below.

1. study _____
   (Par. 9)

2. items for sale _____
   (Par. 11)

3. information storage _____
   (Par. 13)

Check the meaning of the underlined word in each sentence.

4. The park was so crowded there was no room to move.
   ____ part of a house
   ____ space able to be used

5. The ladder had a weak step and was not safe to use.
   ____ rung or stair
   ____ lifting the foot and placing it down in a new place

Learning to Study

A library's card catalog or computer reference system can be used to help you find a book. Books are usually organized three ways in a card catalog or computer reference system. One way is by subject or main topic. Ben wants to know more about robots. Write two subjects he can look up to find books about robots. Do not write *robots* as one of your topics.

1. _____ .

2. _____ .

Reading and Thinking

1. Number the events to show the order in which they happened.
   ____ Ben and Kate ate breakfast.
   ____ Kate said she needs a robot.
   ____ Kate began to clean her room.
   ____ Ben awakened his sister.
   ____ Kate told how robots help people.

Write **T** before the sentences that are true.
Write **F** before the sentences that are false.

2. ____ Robots think like people.
3. ____ Ben and Kate started to clean their rooms.
4. ____ Voices control some robots.
5. ____ Ben explained how robots work.
6. ____ Kate saw a movie about robots.
7. Do you think Ben likes to tease Kate?

   Why or why not? _____

   _____

8. Do you think Kate will ever own a

   robot? Why or why not?_____

   _____

Working with Words

Check the correct meaning of the underlined word.

1. The imperfect machine should be fixed.
   ____ perfect before
   ____ not perfect
   ____ always perfect

2. My sister attends a preschool each day.
   ____ before school
   ____ near school
   ____ after school

Moving Pictures

Have you ever thought about what it takes to make a cartoon?

1   Paul wasn't at all surprised when he got a letter postmarked from California. He knew it was from Ben. They had been friends for a long time. When they went on family vacations, they always sent each other cards or letters. Paul eagerly opened the letter and began to read.

2   Dear Paul,

California is great! I'm having a good time with my grandparents.

3   I wish you could have been with me today. I met someone you would like and admire. His name is Pete, and he's a cartoonist. He is my grandparents' neighbor. Pete draws cartoons for TV shows. He told my grandfather that we could visit him at work while I was here.

4   Pete's studio workroom is a huge room with rows of drawing tables and computers. He showed us something called a "storyboard." The pictures on the board told the basic story of the cartoon he was working on. He said that hundreds of other pictures would be drawn to show all the action when the cartoon was finished.

5   I thought Pete had exaggerated. I asked him if he was sure he meant *hundreds* of pictures. He said twenty-four pictures need to be drawn for each second of a cartoon. That's 1,440 pictures for just one minute. He said fewer pictures make the action look awkward.

6   Pete then told me that the pictures of the lip motions must be drawn to match the words the character will be saying. The cartoon must also match noisy actions, such as doors slamming. Now that I've heard Pete talk, I'll appreciate cartoons much more!

7   I told Pete you have a talent for drawing cartoons. I told him how good you are at making your drawings look as though they're moving. He was pleased to know you are interested in cartooning.

8   Pete gave me one of his work drawings as a souvenir. I decided to send it to you with this letter. I hope you like it.

9   I'll call you when I get home.

Your friend,

Ben

Knowing the Words

Write the words from the story that have the meanings below.

1. marked by the post office _____ (Par. 1)

2. anxiously _____ (Par. 1)

3. made bigger than it really is _____ (Par. 5)

4. something bought or given as a reminder _____ (Par. 8)

A **synonym** is a word with the same or nearly the same meaning as another word. Circle each pair of synonyms.

5. large—huge
6. noisy—quiet
7. talk—hear
8. slam—open
9. ask—inquire

10. awkward—respect
11. admire—respect
12. action—motion
13. picture—drawing
14. friend—enemy

15. Choose one of the synonym pairs above. Use the two synonyms in a sentence. _____

_____

Learning to Study

Complete the following outline. Use the facts in paragraph 5 to complete Part I. Use the facts in paragraph 6 to complete Part II.

I. Pictures for a cartoon
   A. Twenty-four per second
   B. 1,440 per minute
   C. _____

II. Cartoon actions
   A. _____
   B. _____

Reading and Thinking

Circle the word that best completes each sentence.

1. The plow was ____ by a team of horses.
   carried   drawn   pushed

2. The cartoonist drew the ____ of the title.
   letters   souvenirs   sounds

3. Check the sentence that best states the main idea of the story.
   ____ Ben likes to write letters.
   ____ Paul likes to draw cartoons.
   ____ Cartoonists are talented workers.

4. Do you think Ben will encourage Paul to keep drawing cartoons? Why or why not?

_____

_____

Write **T** before the sentences that are true. Write **F** before the sentences that are false.

5. ____ Pete draws cartoons for movies.
6. ____ Ben wrote to Paul from home.
7. ____ Cartoon pictures match lip motions.
8. ____ Each cartoon tells a story.

Working with Words

Check the correct meaning of the underlined word.

1. The girl gave an <u>incorrect</u> answer.
   ____ always correct
   ____ corrected after
   ____ not correct

2. Paula is in the <u>entertainment</u> business.
   ____ one who entertains
   ____ act of entertaining
   ____ entertain before

Surprises at the Zoo

How can animals surprise people?

1   Ben was up bright and early. He was sad that the visit with his grandparents in California was almost over. He wanted to make each day that was left count. He looked out the window and smiled. It was a perfect day to visit the San Diego Zoo. He would meet Ling and a local crew at the zoo this morning. They were going to tape him and a zoo volunteer doing a show with some of the animals as the stars.

2   "Hurry up," Ben shouted for Kate. "The animals won't wait for us."

3   "We'll be on time," said Kate, pretending to check her watch. "Anyway, I'm ready to go. I'll tell Grandma we'll wait for her by the car."

4   After Kate talked with Grandma Wilkins, she waited with Ben outside. Soon Grandma came out of the house, and they started on their way.

5   They parked the car in the zoo lot and followed the main sidewalk through the zoo. Kate suddenly stopped and yelled, "Look!" She pointed high in the air toward a tree. "It's a live teddy bear."

6   Ben and Grandma Wilkins looked up to see a koala in the highest branches. Holding tight to the koala's back was a fuzzy baby.

7   "You're right, Kate. It certainly looks like a teddy bear," said Grandma. She began to read the card in front of the cage. She read that koalas are originally from Australia. They eat only certain kinds of leaves. The zoo grows the trees for the leaves they like right on the zoo grounds. "Now that's real service," said Grandma with a smile. "We'd better get to the Children's Zoo to meet Ling. Good-bye, Teddy," she said, waving to the koala.

8   Ben spotted Ling and the local crew as soon as they reached the Children's Zoo. After he met everyone, they started to tape.

9   Beth, the zoo volunteer, was explaining that volunteers never take care of the big or wild animals. She told Ben that they work with the tame animals, such as the rabbit she was holding. As the tape kept running, the rabbit decided it had been a star long enough and jumped from Beth's arms. Each time someone got close enough to catch it, it would hop away again. The chase was on. Finally, Beth found the rabbit under a bush. It was safe and not even aware of the trouble it had caused.

10   Ben, Ling, and the crew just smiled. "This program will have more action than I thought," said Ling.

11   "It really kept me hopping," said Ben.

Knowing the Words

Write the words from the story that have the meanings below.

1. someone who offers to help _____
   (Par. 1)

2. furry animal that looks like a small bear _____
   (Par. 6)

3. knowing _____
   (Par. 9)

4. A simile compares two things using *like* or *as*. Write the simile in paragraph 7.

   _____

For each pair of meanings below, write one of the homographs that is listed.

    count   spotted   check

5. a. something used as money
   b. to make sure

   _____

6. a. say numbers in order
   b. a person in a high position

   _____

7. a. located
   b. marked with stains

   _____

Working with Words

Read words 1–4 and underline the prefix in each word. Then complete each sentence with one of the words.

1. predate   3. incapable
2. mistrust   4. impersonal

5. I would _____ someone who lied.

6. Because I am not trained, I am _____ of doing the job.

Reading and Thinking

Complete each sentence with the correct word or words from the story.

1. In what city is the zoo located?

   _____

2. What did Kate see in a tree?

   _____

3. Where do koalas come from?

   _____

4. What kind of animals do zoo volunteers

   handle? _____

5. What do you think Ben learned from working with animals for his show?

   _____

6. Do you think Ben will work with animals for his show again? Why or why not?

   _____

   _____

Learning to Study

Complete the following outline. Use the facts from paragraph 7 to complete Part I. Use the facts from paragraph 9 to complete Part II.

I. The koala
    A. Looks like a teddy bear
    B. Comes from Australia

    C. _____

II. Taping Ben's show
    A. Beth began explanation
    B. Rabbit jumped from Beth

    C. _____

    D. _____

Sand Castles

What would you like to build out of sand?

1 "Your vacation to California is almost over, and we haven't taken one trip to the beach," Grandpa Wilkins told Kate. "Let's go today."

2 "That's a great idea, Grandpa," said Kate. "I'll get my swimsuit and towel and ask Ben if he would like to go, too."

3 It didn't take long for Grandpa and the children to get their things together. Soon they were in the car and on their way to the beach. Once the car was parked, they walked to the spot Grandpa picked. While Kate was still dragging a beach bag across the sand, Ben was setting up the chairs. "What's the crowd of people doing down the beach?" Ben asked as he finished with the last chair.

4 "Maybe someone spotted a shark!" shouted Kate.

5 "Let's go see," Grandpa Wilkins suggested.

6 As they neared the group, Kate shouted, "They're making sand castles!"

7 Grandpa laughed and walked closer to the crowd. Then he walked over to a man covered with sand. "George, I'm not surprised to see you playing in the sand again. Ben, Kate, I'd like you to meet Mr. Kirk. He is a champion sand castle builder. Last year he went to the world championship in British Columbia."

8 "I didn't win," Mr. Kirk said with a grin, "but I had a good time. Would you two like to help with this castle?"

9 They both nodded and started to follow Mr. Kirk's directions. They worked from the top down and kept the sand wet so it would hold its shape. Kate smoothed the sand on the side of a tower. Ben used a cone-shaped mold to make pointed tops on the towers.

Mr. Kirk carved an arched entrance, and Grandpa Wilkins brought them water.

10 As they worked, Ben and Kate learned that sometimes people and animal shapes can be built from sand, too. Mr. Kirk told them that a hotel wanted to hold a sand building contest in its ballroom. Everything was fine. Then the owners found out that the sand would weigh six tons! They quickly changed their minds.

11 "Building castles like this one can also be fun," Mr. Kirk said, brushing the sand from his hands. "In 1977 I helped build a castle that was twelve miles long! It stretched all along the Los Angeles coast." He looked toward the water. "You two did a good job. Now you'd better move back from your masterpiece. The tide is coming in."

12 Soon the beach was smooth where the castle had been. Ben and Kate looked at Mr. Kirk and then at each other. They knew they could always build more castles in the sand.

Knowing the Words

Write the words from the story that have the meanings below.

1. winner of a contest _____
   (Par. 7)

2. something used to
   shape things _____
   (Par. 9)

3. rounded _____
   (Par. 9)

4. something made
   with great skill _____
   (Par. 11)

Write the words from the story that would use these abbreviations.

5. CA _____
   (Par. 1)

6. BC _____
   (Par. 7)

In each row, circle the words that belong together.

7. shape   mold   build   blanket

8. sand   hotel   beach   water

Learning to Study

An **index** lists a book's topics in alphabetical order. It also lists page numbers to help you find the topics. Use the index below to answer the questions.

> Sand castles, 4, 9–12
> Sand contests, 13–15
> Sand shapes, 1–8

1. What pages would show different shapes that can be formed from sand?

   _____

2. On what pages can information about

   sand castles be found? _____

3. Under what topic would you look to find facts about a sand building championship?

   _____

Reading and Thinking

1. Check the sentence that best states the main idea of the story.

   ____ Sand can be used to build shapes for contests or for fun.

   ____ There is a certain way to work with sand.

   ____ The beach is the best place to do sand building.

2. Why do you keep the sand wet?_____

   _____

Write **F** before the sentences that are facts. Write **O** before the sentences that are opinions.

3. ____ Everyone can build a sand castle.

4. ____ The weight of sand can be heavy.

5. ____ Sand building contests are fun.

6. ____ The tide can ruin a sand shape.

7. Underline the summary for paragraph 7.

   Ben and Kate meet a champion sand castle builder.

   Mr. Kirk won a world championship.

8. Underline the summary for paragraph 9.

   Grandpa Wilkins helps with the castle.

   Four workers build a sand castle.

Working with Words

Circle the prefix in each underlined word. Then write the underlined word and its meaning.

1. The imperfect towels were on sale.

   _____

2. Mr. Kirk gave Ben a nonfiction book about the history of sand castles.

   _____

A New Tomorrow

What are your ideas about the future?

1 "That was a thrill worth waiting for," Ben exclaimed to his family. They had just gotten off the Space Mountain ride at Disneyland. "Oh look, there's Ling. That must be the guide with her," Ben said as he waved.

2 Ling introduced Jeff, a park guide, to Ben and his family. "I see you've had a chance to see that Walt Disney's words are still true," Jeff offered. "Walt Disney said that this park will never be finished as long as there is imagination left in the world. Those building areas prove his point. There are exciting new plans in the works for Tomorrowland," Jeff added. "Some of the new attractions have been tested at other Disney parks. Other new attractions are old rides that have been made over with a fresh, new look. Let's look around."

3 Mrs. Wilkins told Kate, "Tomorrowland has changed since my first visit. I was about Ben's age, and I loved science. My parents couldn't keep me away from anything that had to do with space travel."

4 Jeff smiled and said, "You must be thinking of Rocket to the Moon and Mission to Mars. Those attractions helped people look to the future. Tomorrowland has always been about new ideas."

5 Kate joined in, "What will be here when I'm Ben's age? Will there be rides that show what life will be like when I grow up?"

6 Ling asked, "How about the things that we can film today?"

7 Jeff motioned for the group to move ahead. The film crew followed. Jeff pointed upward and said to Mrs. Wilkins, "Remember the People Mover. Those tracks will be used for a fast ride called Rocket Rods. Another great ride will help you get a different view of space. Riders will guide starships through a model galaxy of moving planets and stars. A famous thinker from hundreds of years ago gave us that idea. We also want visitors to know that ideas about the future change every day. We keep on dreaming and learning about new things."

8 "I'm dreaming of a nice, cool swim," Mr. Wilkins said.

9 Jeff laughed and said, "Well, you won't be able to swim here. Watching the Wave Maze might cool you off on your next visit. It will be close to Space Mountain. Fountains will send water shooting out of the ground in different patterns."

10 Ling told Ben that they had filmed enough for the day. "Go ahead," she said to Ben. "I know you can't wait to get back on Space Mountain."

11 Ben's dad ran ahead. "I'll blast off before you," he said.

Knowing the Words

Write the words from the story that have the meanings below.

1. thinking of new things _____
   (Par. 2)

2. times to come _____
   (Par. 4)

3. used arm movements _____
   (Par. 7)

Check the meaning of the underlined word in each sentence.

4. I bought a <u>watch</u> at the jewelry store.
   ____ something used to keep time
   ____ look

5. He had to <u>board</u> the tour bus twice.
   ____ get on something
   ____ a piece of wood

Learning to Study

Many words have more than one part of speech. Some dictionaries give definitions of each part of speech in a separate entry. Symbols for two parts of speech are *n = noun* and *v = verb*. Use the dictionary entries below to answer the questions.

¹**building** /bil'ding/ *n* something built
²**building** /bil'ding/ *v* make or put together

1. What part of speech is the word in the first entry? _____

2. What does the word *building* mean when it is used as a verb?

   _____

3. Number the words in alphabetical order.
   ____ scrap   ____ seal
   ____ scream   ____ scratch
   ____ sandy   ____ scramble

Reading and Thinking

1. Number the events to show the order in which they happened.
   ____ Mrs. Wilkins told about her visit.
   ____ Ben's father teased Ben.
   ____ Ben met the guide.
   ____ Jeff talked about the new rides.
   ____ Ben's family enjoyed a ride.

2. Check the sentence that best states the main idea of this story.
   ____ Ben likes Space Mountain.
   ____ Tomorrowland is always changing.
   ____ Rocket Rods will be a fast ride.

Circle the word that best completes each sentence.

3. The first ____ of the film is exciting.

   scene   approach   cover

4. On Sundays, my brother ____ his boat to his favorite fishing spot.

   throws   rows   recognizes

5. Check the reason the author probably wrote this story.
   ____ to tell about Walt Disney
   ____ to tell about Tomorrowland
   ____ to tell about fun rides

Working with Words

Use two words from each sentence to make a compound word. Write the compound word in the blank.

1. Kate must wear her glasses in the sun.

   _____

2. The child felt the earth start to quake.

   _____

Airplane Pioneers

Could you write a school report about your hobby?

1   Robert had been building and collecting model airplanes for a few years. He decided to write his school report about his favorite subject, flying. Today he sat staring at his collection as he tried to think of the facts he wanted to include in this assignment. He had read many books about airplanes.

2   Robert started to take notes as he thought. He wrote that Kitty Hawk, North Carolina, was where Wilbur and Orville Wright had the first successful airplane flight in 1903. The Wright brothers got many of their ideas from watching birds fly! They noticed that birds raise and lower the front edges of their wings when they fly. That's how they control their flight. The Wrights tried out this theory. They designed a glider with wings they could move. That worked so well, they built an airplane with wings that moved.

3   Robert put down his pen and picked up a piece of paper. He quickly folded it into a paper airplane. Then he threw it into the air. He watched as it crashed against his bedroom wall. The wings on that plane did not move, he thought. It could fly only in a straight line until it crashed. That's what happened to some of the earlier designs of the Wrights.

4   Robert took his pen and began writing again. He wanted to include how the Wright brothers tested their designs themselves. He remembered that they flipped a coin to see which brother would make that first flight. Robert wrote that Wilbur won the toss, but he didn't make the first flight. A wing tip broke before the plane got off the ground. It took three days to fix the damage. Since Wilbur had tried once, it was now Orville's turn. The plane flew for twelve seconds! Robert planned to include that fact. He knew his classmates would find it hard to believe, since today's airplanes stay in the air for hours.

5   He also wanted to include some facts about two other airplane pioneers. Both Louis Blériot and Harriet Quimby flew across the English Channel. Quimby made her flight in a plane made of wood, cloth, and bicycle wheels. Both flights covered more than twenty-one miles. This was a great improvement when compared to Orville Wright's flight of only one hundred twenty feet!

6   Robert stopped writing and read over his notes. He thought he had used facts that would make his report good. As he started to write, he wondered. Would he ever do anything someone would write a school report about?

Knowing the Words

Write the words from the story that have the meanings below.

1. having a good result _____
(Par. 2)

2. idea _____
(Par. 2)

3. a type of airplane
with no motor _____
(Par. 2)

A word that means the opposite of another word is an **antonym.** Write the pair of antonyms from each sentence.

4. The wings of the plane were designed to be straight, but when they moved they looked crooked.

_____

5. The Wrights repaired the plane after it was damaged during the flight.

_____

Learning to Study

Use this chart to answer the questions.

Wright Brothers' First Flight		
	Orville's Flight	Wilbur's Flight
Distance	120 feet	852 feet
Time	12 seconds	59 seconds
Date	December 17	December 17

1. Who flew the longest distance?_____

2. How much time did the shorter flight take? _____

3. What was the distance of Orville's flight? _____

Reading and Thinking

1. Check the sentence that best states the main idea of the story.

_____ Robert wants to be a pilot.

_____ Robert writes a report about famous pilots.

_____ Robert wants to design planes.

2. Why didn't Wilbur Wright make the first flight?_____

_____

_____

3. Do you think airplanes will continue to be improved? Why or why not? _____

_____

Write **F** before the sentences that are facts. Write **O** before the sentences that are opinions.

4. _____ The first successful airplane flight was in 1903.

5. _____ The Wright brothers had the best plane.

6. _____ A woman flew more than twenty-one miles across the English Channel.

7. _____ The Wright brothers are the most important men in the history of flight.

Working with Words

Fill in each blank with the possessive form of the word in parentheses.

1. Some _____ ideas have helped to improve modern flight. (women)

2. The _____ airplane designs were judged. (men)

Mountain of Fire

Would you ever fly over a volcano?

1   "How were your winter vacations?" Ling asked. She smiled at the cast members. They were meeting with her to plan new shows for *Just for Openers.* "I know Ben went to California. Did anyone else go anywhere?"

2   "I did," said Carmen. "My family and I went to visit my brother in Washington. While we were there, he took me for a helicopter ride over Mount St. Helens!"

3   "I'd never fly over a volcano," said Cindy.

4   "My brother, Joe, trusted the pilot," Carmen said. "He's a scientist and knew we would be safe, but it was still scary at first. When we flew inside the crater of the volcano, I *did* close my eyes!"

5   "Was the volcano full of fire?" Ben asked.

6   "No, it's quiet now," she told him, "but the whole top of it looks like part of the moon. It's all black and there are no trees or grass."

7   "Was Joe there when Mount St. Helens exploded in 1980?" Ling asked.

8   Carmen nodded. "He and the other scientists were studying small earthquakes near the mountain. Joe said that the earthquakes were caused by huge plates of rock shifting deep under the mountain. Sometimes the edge of one plate gets trapped under the other. Then heat from inside the earth makes the bottom plate start to melt. Joe said that when that happens, gas forms and pressure builds up until the volcano explodes. And that's just what happened. Mount St. Helens exploded!" Carmen continued. "The force of the explosion was like a bomb. It knocked over thousands of trees. The heat from the explosion melted the ice on the mountaintop. The boiling water mixed with

dirt and ash. It poured down the mountain in hot rivers of mud. When the mud reached the closest river, it heated the water there to ninety degrees. All the fish died."

9   "Did lava come out of the volcano?" Laurie asked.

10   "Not this time," Carmen told her. "Joe said when a volcano explodes suddenly, the melted rock shooting out cools off quickly. It turns into tons of ash instead of lava. Towns five hundred miles away had to clean up ash that was a half-inch thick."

11   "How can anything grow or live on the mountain with all that ash?" asked Ben.

12   "I don't know," Carmen said, smiling, "but Joe showed me where ferns and flowers are growing. We even saw deer tracks. The mountain has a new life!"

Photograph by Gary Braasch

Knowing the Words

Write the words from the story that have the meanings below.

1. hole around the
    opening of a volcano _____
    (Par. 4)

2. blast _____
    (Par. 8)

Check the meaning of the underlined homograph as it is used in the sentence.

3. Carmen wanted to <u>fly</u> to Washington.

    _____ an insect

    _____ to travel by plane

4. The records had to be kept in the office <u>safe</u> until the meeting.

    _____ special box for valuables

    _____ free from harm

5. Write the simile found in paragraph 8.

    _____

    _____

Learning to Study

Use the entry below to answer the questions.

trunk/trungk/*n* **1** the main part of a tree; **2** a box with a lid used when traveling

1. Write the first definition listed in the

    entry. _____

2. Underline the sentence in which *trunk* has the same meaning as the second definition.

    The trunk was packed for the trip.

    The bark fell from the trunk of the tree.

3. Write a sentence that uses *trunk* meaning "the main part of a tree."

    _____

Reading and Thinking

1. Number the events to show the order in which they happened.

    _____ Ash from the volcano was found hundreds of miles away.

    _____ Plates of rock shifted under the mountain.

    _____ The volcano exploded.

    _____ Pressure built up as gas formed.

    _____ Animals and trees were destroyed.

Circle the word that best completes each sentence.

2. The owner wanted to _____ the shop.

    trust   cut   close

3. I like to _____ in that chair.

    rock   knock   tracks

4. The railroad _____ were fixed.

    pilots   mountains   tracks

5. How does Cindy feel about flying over a

    volcano?_____

    _____

6. Write the name of the character these words describe.

    trusting   excited   curious

    _____

Working with Words

Fill in each blank with the possessive form of the word in parentheses.

1. The _____ journals were discussed at the annual meeting in Boston. (scientists)

2. _____ licenses are to be bought before Monday. (pilots)

Letters

What idea would you suggest for a show?

1   The studio meeting room was very quiet. Ling thought the meeting with the cast of *Just for Openers* had gone well. Many of the show's viewers had sent in letters with suggestions for future shows. Ling and the cast had read the letters. Some of the ideas were funny. One of the viewers suggested a show about hogs. The viewer thought Ben could go to a hog-calling contest. Ling smiled to herself thinking of Ben calling a hog. She was beginning to read one of the last letters when the meeting room door opened. Laurie walked into the room and sat down next to Ling.

2   "Hi, Ling," Laurie said. "My mom is late picking me up, and she asked if I could wait with you until she gets to the studio."

3   "That's fine," said Ling. "It's nice to have some company. I was just reading another letter. What did you think about some of the ideas?"

4   "I really like the idea about the cooking school for kids. I think the juggling contest could be interesting, too. The kids who watch the show had some good ideas," Laurie said, smiling.

5   Ling glanced over the letter she had opened. "Here's an idea we could use. It goes with the juggling idea you liked," she said to Laurie. "What about a show on a special kind of college—a clown college?"

6   "That sounds like the kind of school I'd like to go to," said Laurie, laughing. "What does the letter say about this clown college?"

7   Ling answered Laurie's question. "The writer says that Ringling Brothers and Barnum and Bailey Circus opened the Clown College. It is in Venice, Florida, the winter home of the circus. The school was started to train clowns for their circus," Ling read.

8   "I never thought about it. I guess a circus would have to work hard to get good clowns," Laurie said.

9   "Yes, I guess as many as one thousand people want to attend each year. However, the school can take only thirty. After you get in, there is no guarantee that you will be hired by the circus. The students are taught to dance, to do stunts, to juggle, to mime, and to put on makeup. The letter explains that the clown students must perform their acts for their teachers. After doing that they can graduate from the school," Ling told Laurie as she finished reading. "I think the clown college would be a great place to tape a show."

10   "It sounds as if making people laugh is serious business," said Laurie. "The people don't clown around in that school."

Knowing the Words

Write the words from the story that have the meanings below.

1. promise _____
(Par. 9)

2. tricks that are practiced _____
(Par. 9)

3. to throw and catch many
things at one time _____
(Par. 9)

Check the meaning of the underlined word in each sentence.

4. Some schools <u>train</u> students to act.

____ teach

____ a type of transportation

5. My friend took a <u>course</u> at night school to learn acting.

____ direction or path

____ class taken to learn

Learning to Study

You can use a computer reference system or a card catalog to help you find a book you want. One way books are organized in a card catalog or computer reference system is by title. Use the information below to answer questions.

CALL NO:	791.335
AUTHOR:	Stone, Mary
MAIN TITLE:	Clowns and the Circus
PUBLISHER:	Greenwillow, 1994

1. What is the title of the book? _____

_____

2. What is the last name of the author?

_____

Reading and Thinking

1. Who wrote the letters Ling was reading?

_____

2. What was one suggestion for Ben's show?

_____

3. What show ideas did Laurie like?

_____

_____

4. Where is the Clown College?

_____

5. Check the sentence that best states the main idea of the story.

____ Viewers' ideas are discussed.

____ Juggling is a difficult skill.

____ You can learn how to be a clown.

6. Why was Laurie at the studio late? _____

_____

7. Do you think Ling will use the idea about the clown college for the show?

Why or why not? _____

_____

Working with Words

Fill in each blank with the possessive form of the word in parentheses.

1. The _____ letters expressed many good ideas for the TV show. (viewers)

2. Some of the _____ acts were judged today. (jugglers)

3. The _____ costumes are chosen with care. (clowns)

55

Underwater Fun

What could you see in the ocean underwater?

1   Both Ben and Kate heard the sound at the same time. It could mean only one thing. The mail had just been delivered to the house. They jumped up from the kitchen table and raced through the house to the front door. Scattered on the floor was the mail for the day. Both of them reached down and scooped up a handful of envelopes. They were looking for something special. Mrs. Wilkins was in Florida attending a nurses' meeting. She had phoned Kate and Ben the night before and told them she had sent a letter.

2   "This has to be it," said Kate. She waved an envelope over her head. "Dad, Mom's letter is here!" she shouted, as they both ran back into the kitchen.

3   "Open the letter and read what your mom wrote," said Mr. Wilkins. "She said she was enjoying her stay with the Smiths. They were such good neighbors. It was nice

of them to invite your mom to stay with them while she was in Florida."

4   As her dad was talking, Kate opened the letter. A picture fell from the envelope and landed on the table. Ben looked at the picture and laughed. "This looks like a picture of someone from outer space!" he said. "Read the letter, Kate. I'm sure Mom explains the picture."

5   Kate started to read. The letter explained that the girl in the picture was Sue Smith. She had just finished a course in snorkeling and was wearing typical snorkeling equipment. She had a long, black tube sticking out of her mouth, a black face mask, and big flippers. She looked strange. Mrs. Wilkins wrote that Sue had learned how to swim facedown in the water and breathe through the snorkel.

6   Kate stopped reading and asked, "Why would Sue want to float on top of the water, with her face down?"

7   Mr. Wilkins smiled. "People don't snorkel much in Chicago. Around Florida, however, the ocean is full of colorful fish. The coral just off the coast is beautiful, too."

8   "What happens if the top end of the snorkel goes underwater?" asked Kate.

9   "The tube will fill with water. If you don't blow the water out, you'll end up with a mouthful of it," explained Mr. Wilkins. "Remember, Mom wrote that Sue took lessons. She had to learn how to breathe through the snorkel. She also had to pass several swimming and water safety tests."

10   Kate finished reading the letter and started to laugh. "Mom says she is going to a beginners' snorkeling class. I hope she sends us her picture from class. I want to see how Mom looks as a creature from outer space."

Knowing the Words

Write the words from the story that have the meanings below.

1. lifted _____
   (Par. 1)

2. a water activity _____
   (Par. 5)

3. usual kind or type _____
   (Par. 5)

4. tube used to breathe
   underwater _____
   (Par. 5)

A word that means the opposite of another word is an **antonym.** Find an antonym in the story for each of the words below.

5. ordinary _____
   (Par. 1)

6. leave _____
   (Par. 3)

7. sink _____
   (Par. 6)

Learning to Study

Mrs. Wilkins used this schedule to help her choose her flight home to Chicago. Read the schedule and answer the questions.

Central Airlines Orlando to Chicago		
Flight	Leaves	Arrives
602	9:30 A.M.	10:30 A.M.
348	1:00 P.M.	2:00 P.M.
521	7:30 P.M.	8:30 P.M.

1. This schedule is for flights from Orlando to what city? _____

2. Which flight could she take if she wants to travel in the morning? _____

3. If she takes Flight 348, when will she arrive? _____

4. Can she be home before 10:00 A.M.?

   _____

Reading and Thinking

Circle the word that best completes each sentence.

1. The strong ____ carried the swimmer toward the shore.

   snorkel   wave   fish

2. We decorated the ____ for the parade.

   table   scoop   float

3. Why did Sue take lessons before she went snorkeling? _____

   _____

4. Why should you blow water out of the snorkel? _____

   _____

Write **X** before the groups of words that describe Chicago. Write **Y** before the groups of words that describe Florida.

5. ____ where Mrs. Wilkins visited

6. ____ home of the Wilkins family

7. ____ is not on the ocean

8. ____ has coral off the coast

9. ____ good place for snorkeling

Working with Words

Write a compound word using two words from each sentence.

1. A boat that runs on steam is called a

   _____.

2. A bell that you ring at a door is called a

   _____.

3. Something used to mark a place in a

   book is called a _____.

The Other World of Disney

Is there anything else at Disney World besides rides and shows?

1   "I had a wonderful time in Florida. I missed all of you though," Mrs. Wilkins told her family. She had just returned on Monday from a nurses' meeting. "I learned so much at the meeting. I enjoyed my stay with the Smiths, too. I've missed them since they moved to Florida. I also learned something about Disney World that might appeal to you, Ben," said Mrs. Wilkins, smiling.

2   "I'm interested, Mom. I want to see the shows, ride the rides, and see all of my favorite characters," Ben said.

3   "I knew that, Ben," said his mom. "What I learned was that Disney World has even more to offer, especially for your age group and older."

4   "What about me?" asked Kate sadly.

5   "Don't worry, Kate. There is enough for you to enjoy without joining this program," Mrs. Wilkins replied.

6   "What program is that, Mom?" asked Ben.

7   "Disney World offers different programs for your age group, Ben. You could learn about energy. You could go backstage at the Disney shows, or you could choose what Tess Smith chose to do," his mom explained.

8   Ben knew that Tess was the oldest girl in the Smith family. "What did Tess choose?" he asked.

9   "Tess told me that Disney World has a nature preserve," Mrs. Wilkins explained. "It spreads over thousands of acres. Only special tours, like the nature program, can go in there. Tess and her group spent the day in the preserve. They used binoculars to watch birds and alligators. They were even given cameras to take pictures of things they found interesting," continued his mom. "Tess told me the thing she learned to appreciate the most was the bugs!"

10   "She learned to like bugs?" Kate asked. She wrinkled her nose in disgust.

11   Mrs. Wilkins laughed at her daughter. "Tess said all the kids were complaining about the bugs. Their guide asked what would happen if all the bugs left."

12   "The tour would be more fun, right?" Ben suggested.

13   "No, there wouldn't be a tour if that happened. Tess said she learned that the birds and fish that eat the bugs would leave. If that happened, the alligators and other wildlife would soon disappear as well," Mrs. Wilkins told the children.

14   "A small change can cause a big change in the preserve," said Mr. Wilkins.

15   "When Disney World was built it wasn't made just for people," said Ben. "It was made for the world of wildlife, too!"

Knowing the Words

Write the words from the story that have the meanings below.

1. interest _____
(Par. 1)

2. area used
for protection _____
(Par. 9)

3. units of land _____
(Par. 9)

Write a word from the story that matches each of these abbreviations.

4. FL _____

5. Mon. _____

In each row, circle the words that belong together.

6. rides   shows   games   meeting

7. camera   birds   bugs   alligators

8. friends   family   tour   neighbors

Learning to Study

Tess had some questions about wildlife after she'd spent the day at the nature preserve. She checked a book out from the library. Read part of her book's index and answer the questions.

> Alligators, 18–19
> Birds, 1–16, 33–67
> Insects, 68–102
> Nature preserves, 103–132

1. Under what topic could Tess look to find facts about bugs? _____

2. What topic is covered in two different places in the book? _____

3. On what pages might Tess find facts about the nature preserve at Disney World? _____

Reading and Thinking

1. Check the sentence that best states the main idea of this story.

____ Meetings in Florida are fun.

____ Ben will travel to Disney World.

____ Disney World has special programs.

2. Write one thing that might change in your neighborhood if all the birds left.

_____

_____

3. Check the reason the author probably wrote this story.

____ to tell about wildlife

____ to tell about a nature preserve within an amusement park

____ to tell about energy

Write **F** before the sentences that are facts. Write **O** before the sentences that are opinions.

4. ____ The nature preserve at Disney World covers hundreds of acres.

5. ____ Everyone would like the nature program.

6. ____ Binoculars can be used to watch birds more closely.

7. ____ Bugs aren't good for anything.

Working with Words

Fill in each blank with the possessive form of the word in parentheses.

1. The _____ animals are fun to watch. (preserves)

2. Some _____ leaves are food for the bugs. (trees)

3. _____ habits are studied at the nature preserve. (birds)

Space Camp

What would you do at a Space Camp?

1 Ben remembered when his teacher had given him the information about the Space Camp. At the time, Ben had been so busy that he just stuffed the papers into his locker. He didn't think about Space Camp at all. Then, a few days later, he found himself needing new ideas for the show. After reading about the camp, he wanted to go there. He talked it over with his parents and then with Ling. They all thought it would be a good experience for him. They also agreed that it would make a great show.

2 "I can see the top of a rocket sticking up above the trees! We're getting close!" Ben said. He and his dad would soon land in Huntsville, Alabama. Then Ben would spend a week at Space Camp. Ling would arrive on Thursday to tape part of Ben's stay at the camp for his show.

3 When Ben and his dad got to the Space Camp, Ben checked in at the new training center where he would be staying. It was modeled after the training center for astronauts in Houston. "I wonder how I would be feeling if I were really here to learn to be an astronaut," thought Ben. "This is going to be so exciting."

4 Once they had checked in at the camp, Ben and his dad had time to see the world's largest space museum. It is called The Space and Rocket Center. In an hour, they were in the museum. It was filled with real spacecraft.

5 Ben peered into the porthole of *Apollo 16*. Three astronauts had traveled in it to the moon. "It's so small and crowded," Ben said. "I couldn't travel back to Chicago in this, much less go to the moon!"

6 "Everything the astronauts needed was designed to fit into that small space," said his dad.

7 A boy about Ben's age, who was standing nearby, overheard them and said, "Are you here for Space Camp, too?"

8 Ben nodded. "My name is Jim," the boy continued. "I flew in from Canada with two younger classmates. My seventh grade science teacher told us about this place, and now I'm glad she did."

9 Ben introduced himself and his dad to Jim. "Can you tell us what else we should see in the museum?" asked Ben.

10 "You'd like the moonship," said Jim. "It lets you feel three times the normal gravity. That is what the astronauts feel during a launch. The moonship is neat, but the movies are my favorite. The screen surrounds you, and when a launch is shown the sound is like thunder. Clouds of smoke seem to billow up around you. It's great!"

11 Ben smiled. "If Space Camp is as much fun as the museum, it'll be a great week."

Knowing the Words

Write the words from the story that have the meanings below.

1. looked _____
   (Par. 5)

2. force of the earth _____
   (Par. 10)

3. act of sending off _____
   (Par. 10)

A **synonym** is a word with the same or nearly the same meaning as another word. Circle each pair of synonyms.

4. close—near   7. teacher—instructor

5. part—whole   8. above—beneath

6. space—area   9. filled—empty

Match the word in the first column with its abbreviation.

10. ____ Alabama   **a.** Thurs.

11. ____ Canada   **b.** AL

12. ____ Thursday   **c.** CAN

Learning to Study

This is part of an application for Space Camp. Read the application form and answer the questions. Then fill out the form.

Name			
	Last	First	Middle
Address			
	Number	Street	
	City	State	Zip
Birth date			
	Day	Month	Year

1. What part of the name is written last?

   _____

2. Does the application ask for facts about

   the day you were born? _____

3. What two things are written on the first

   address line? _____

Reading and Thinking

1. Number the events to show the order in which they happened.

   ____ Ben was told about the moonship.

   ____ Ben saw *Apollo 16*.

   ____ Ben read about Space Camp.

   ____ Ben got permission to go to Space Camp.

   ____ Ben went to the new training center.

Circle the word that best completes each sentence.

2. The first few pages of my notebook kept ____ together when I turned them.

   spending   sticking   training

3. The group leader ____ the space suit so we could see how it looked.

   modeled   traveled   talked

4. Do you think Ben enjoyed the museum?

   Why or why not? _____

   _____

5. If he could, do you think Ben would like to travel in space? Why or why not?

   _____

   _____

Working with Words

Fill in each blank with the possessive form of the word in parentheses.

1. Ben thought the _____ cabins were very small. (astronauts)

2. Both _____ collections interest the tourists. (museums)

3. While he was gone, Ben read his

   _____ letters. (classmates)

A Day to Remember

Would you like to walk and work in space?

1   Everyone was laughing as they watched Joy, one of the campers in Ben's group at Space Camp. She was sitting in a chair that made her have a feeling of weightlessness, which is the same feeling people experience on the moon.

2   "How are you feeling, Joy?" asked Jean, their team leader.

3   "I feel as if I'm floating on air. I could stay here all day," said Joy, giggling.

4   "Sorry, Joy. You have to come back down to earth. Ken and Meg have to take their turns in the micro-gravity chair," said Jean.

5   The chair was lowered from the air and Joy joined the rest of the campers as Ken took his turn.

6   "I never did anything like that before in my life," said Joy to Ben and the others.

7   "During this week I've done a lot of things I've never done before," Meg agreed. "This is the first time I ever built a rocket, and I never ate space food until yesterday."

8   As the class talked, they watched the other two campers try out the chair. For the rest of the day, the campers would be working with space equipment. They would learn about the kind that helps astronauts learn how to walk on the moon and work in space. All of these programs were a part of Micro Gravity Day.

9   Soon all the campers were finished. Jean then said, "Let me tell you about another piece of equipment. This machine is designed to train astronauts to steady their spacecraft if it starts to tumble out of control. I'll demonstrate it for you."

10   Then Jean strapped herself into a seat surrounded by a steel frame. One of the other group leaders turned on the machine. The seat started to spin and tumble in all directions inside the frame, and soon Jean was just a blur of color. As Ben watched, he whispered to Ken, "Wow! I'm glad we don't have to do that."

11   "When the machine finally stopped tumbling and spinning, Jean looked at the group. "Please stand still," she said.

12   The campers just laughed. "We aren't moving at all, Jean," Ken said.

13   A short time later, the class had changed into their swimsuits and were standing beside a pool. Jean gave each of them a face mask and tools. She pointed to some objects at the bottom of the pool. Then she asked each of the campers to do some tasks underwater while the tools floated around in the water. The campers learned how hard working in space could be.

14   At dinner, all the campers talked about what they had done during the day. They all agreed that learning about space was an experience that was out of this world!

Knowing the Words

Write the words from the story that have the meanings below.

1. condition of having
   no force of gravity _____
   (Par. 1)

2. not clear _____
   (Par. 10)

Check the meaning of the homograph as it is used in the sentence.

3. We watched a TV program about space.

   ____ printed facts about a performance

   ____ a scheduled show

4. The girl had to rest after the long trip.

   ____ relax

   ____ what is left over

Learning to Study

Write the number of the encyclopedia volume that would have the most information for each topic. Remember that a person is listed by his or her last name.

Vol. 1	Vol. 2	Vol. 3	Vol. 4	Vol. 5	Vol. 6	Vol. 7
A–C	D–F	G–J	K–M	N–Q	R–T	U–Z

1. ____ John Glenn
2. ____ astronauts
3. ____ Sally Ride
4. ____ planets

Read the weather forecast below. Then answer the questions.

> Weather Forecast
> for the Los Angeles area
>
> —Cloudy and cooler Friday
> —Low temperature Friday around 50
> —Wind and rain Saturday
> —High temperature 65 Saturday

5. What day will be windy? _____

6. How cool will it be Friday? _____

7. Will the sky be clear Saturday? _____

Reading and Thinking

1. Check the sentence that best states the main idea of the story.

   ____ The campers learn about gravity.

   ____ The campers taste space food.

   ____ A spacecraft can go out of control.

2. Why did the seat in the frame spin in all directions? _____

   _____

   _____

3. Why was it hard to work underwater?

   _____

4. Do you think Joy likes to try new things? Why or why not? _____

   _____

Write **C** before the words that describe what the campers did. Write **J** before the words that describe what Jean did.

5. ____ sat in a chair and felt weightless

6. ____ tumbled inside a steel frame

7. ____ worked in a pool with tools

8. ____ gave out face masks

9. ____ pointed to objects underwater

10. ____ felt dizzy

Working with Words

Write a compound word using two words in each sentence.

1. A ball that you kick is a _____.

2. A berry that is blue is a _____.

3. A storm of snow is a _____.

4. A craft in outer space is a _____.

Mission Control

Would you like to send something into space?

1 "I think this will be the most exciting day at Space Camp!" Ben said. He was with his friends at breakfast on Friday. "I remember when I first read the information about the Space Camp. I thought Space Shuttle Mission Day sounded the best of all the days. All I knew was that a shuttle is a kind of spacecraft. I know we'll learn more today."

2 "I've learned so much already," Meg said. "Before I came here, I didn't even know how a rocket worked. That's why I was so surprised when the rocket I built went the highest!"

3 "I liked designing the space station," Ken added. "We had some good ideas, and some ideas that were off the wall!"

4 "Well, the ideas are for outer space!" laughed Ben. "Do you think Marshall Space Flight Center might use our ideas when they build the first real space station?"

5 "Maybe," Meg said, "but I have a down-to-earth question. Are you really on TV each week, Ben?"

6 Ben smiled. Ling and a crew from Huntsville had taped the campers launching their rockets on Thursday. After more than three years on *Just for Openers,* Ben hardly noticed the cameras anymore.

7 Before Ben could explain, Jean, their team leader, came into the room.

8 "We need two crews today," she began. "One will pilot the shuttle. The other will direct the flight from Mission Control."

9 She divided the twelve campers into two groups. Ben's group hurried to Mission Control. After he got there, Ben sat down in front of a panel of dials and buttons. He put on the headphones. Then a strange thing happened. For a minute Ben imagined he was actually in charge of a space shuttle. Soon he would give the commands that would fly the shuttle to one of the space stations.

10 "Ben, did you hear me?" Ken asked.

11 "Oh, sure, Ken!" Ben said quickly as he realized he was just supposed to be pretending. "Let's check everything the way we practiced this week."

12 Ling directed the crew to tape Ben as he watched the shuttle crew on a TV screen. Then the countdown began. Finally, they got the signal. It was a "go."

13 Suddenly the room was filled with the thundering noise of a real launch. The campers in Ben's group congratulated each other on the success of the launch.

14 As the "flight" continued, there was a problem with the fuel line. Both crews worked together to solve it. At last Mission Control "landed" the shuttle safely.

15 "What a great way to end my stay at Space Camp," thought Ben.

Photograph courtesy of NASA

Knowing the Words

Write the words from the story that have the meanings below.

1. a type of spacecraft _____
(Par. 1)

2. knobs that turn _____
(Par. 9)

3. expressed happiness about
success of something _____
(Par. 13)

4. something used
to produce energy _____
(Par. 14)

Draw a line under the homophone that correctly completes each sentence.

5. Joy could ____ the loud noises.

   (here, hear)

6. We were at camp for five ____.

   (daze, days)

7. Idioms are groups of words that have special meanings. Write the idiom found in paragraph 3.

   _____

Learning to Study

A library book can be listed in the card catalog or computer reference system by the **author.** Books are entered by the author's last name. Use the following information to answer the questions.

CALL NO:	473.02
AUTHOR:	Kirk, Roberta
MAIN TITLE:	The Worlds of Space
PUBLISHER:	James Press, 1993

1. What is the author's name? _____

2. Under what name would this author be entered in a computer reference system or a card catalog? _____

Reading and Thinking

Circle the word that best completes each sentence.

1. A ____ of experts discussed the ideas and made a fair decision.

   control   command   panel

2. The captain took ____ of the ship.

   charge   information   practice

Write **T** before the sentences that are true.
Write **F** before the sentences that are false.

3. ____ Meg built and launched a rocket.

4. ____ Ben helped to pilot the shuttle.

5. ____ The crew taped Ben at Space Camp.

6. ____ The flight had no problems.

7. Write a sentence from the story that tells you the campers at Mission Control were happy with the launch.

   _____

   _____

   _____

8. In what way could space launches

   change in the future? _____

   _____

Working with Words

Underline the word in each sentence that has a prefix. Then write the meaning of the underlined word in the blank.

1. The project was incomplete because the crew had not followed the rules.

   _____

2. His inattention to time made him late.

   _____

Monkey Business

How does Jane Goodall help people learn?

1 The cast of *Just for Openers* sat and looked at each other. They needed one more idea for a show. Suddenly Cindy sat up straight. "I've got an idea," she said. "Why don't we do a story on Jane Goodall's work?"

2 "Who is Jane Goodall? Why would her work be a good idea for our show?" Ben asked.

3 "I read about her in the newspaper," Cindy said. "She does research in Africa. Since 1960, she has been studying the habits of chimpanzees. It was hard for Jane to get the chimps to trust her. It was two years before some of the chimps would come to her camp for bananas," Cindy went on. "Her study of the chimps has led to two important discoveries. She learned that chimps use things from their surroundings to make simple tools. She also learned that chimps eat meat. Before, it was believed that chimps ate only fruits and vegetables. Neither of these facts was known before Jane's study began," Cindy explained.

4 Robert spoke up, "It's nice to dream about a trip to Africa. We know that we can't go there. If Jane Goodall is so famous, we won't have a chance to learn from her. How about another idea?"

5 Ling looked up from her computer screen and said, "Not so fast, Robert. Let's think about this idea a little more. Jane Goodall has done a lot of speaking about her work since the 1980s. She also has a program that uses hands-on activities to teach kids and adults."

6 "That doesn't sound much like a program about chimpanzees," Ben said. "What else does that say?"

7 Ling explained as she read, "The Roots and Shoots program teaches about three issues. First, it helps teach an understanding of the environment. Other activities help people learn about animal and human concerns. If people learn about these things, there is a better chance for all animals to survive. I guess that's where the chimpanzees come in."

8 Cindy asked, "Where would we go to film one of these programs in action? I'd like to see the activities that kids our age would do."

9 "Let me call this number and see where we could film a Roots and Shoots youth program," Ling said. "I'm sure we'll have a choice of places to go. If you're lucky, you may even get to participate in one of these groups. If I know this cast, this idea will lead to more than one show."

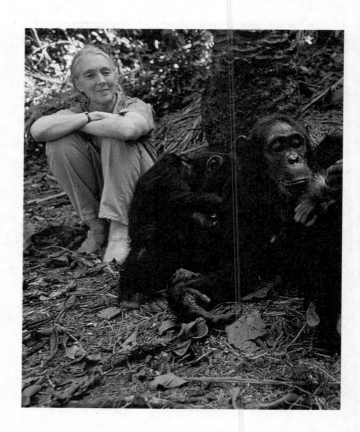

Knowing the Words

Write the words from the story that have the meanings below.

1. studies _____
   (Par. 3)
2. problems or subjects _____
   (Par. 7)
3. take part in _____
   (Par. 9)

A **synonym** is a word with the same or nearly the same meaning as another word. Write the pair of synonyms from each sentence.

4. The class listed their thoughts on the board, and the ideas were voted on.

   _____

5. After we watched the movie, the artist showed us how the film was made.

   _____

Learning to Study

1. Complete the following outline. Use paragraph 3 to complete Part I. Use paragraph 7 to complete Part II.

   I. Studying the chimps
      A. Worked to build trust

      B. _____

      C. _____

   II. Teaching through Roots and Shoots
      A. Teaches about the environment

      B. _____

      C. _____

2. Number the words below in alphabetical order.

   ____ blame   ____ believe

   ____ black   ____ bike

   ____ badge   ____ blank

Reading and Thinking

1. Check the sentence that best states the main idea of the story.

   ____ Jane Goodall works in Africa.

   ____ Goodall studies and teaches.

   ____ Goodall started Roots and Shoots.

2. Number the events to show the order in which they happened.

   ____ Goodall spoke about chimps.

   ____ Jane Goodall went to Africa.

   ____ Goodall learned chimps make tools.

   ____ Goodall started Roots and Shoots.

   ____ Goodall began studying chimps.

Write **F** before the sentences that are facts. Write **O** before the sentences that are opinions.

3. ____ Chimps eat fruits, vegetables, and meat.

4. ____ Goodall studied chimps in 1960.

5. ____ Chimps are afraid of people.

6. What do you think Jane Goodall wants people to learn from Roots and Shoots?

   _____

Working with Words

Check the correct meaning of the underlined word.

1. Do not <u>misuse</u> the new equipment.

   ____ use badly

   ____ use before

   ____ use often

2. It is <u>impolite</u> to interrupt the speaker.

   ____ very polite

   ____ not polite

   ____ often polite

Days of Old

Would you like to visit the past?

1   Carmen thought about her first year on the TV show *Just for Openers.* She smiled. She remembered how nervous she was when she met the cast and crew for the first time. Now she felt relaxed working with them. She loved being on the show.

2   Carmen loved working on *Just for Openers,* too. Yet, she had never felt sure enough to offer ideas for the show. She had one idea she had thought about for a long time. She wanted to do a show about the Renaissance Festival in Sterling Forest, Tuxedo, New York. She had gone to the festival herself and loved it. So one day, she mentioned the idea to Ling.

3   "I think our viewers would like something that is so different," Carmen said. Ling asked to hear more.

4   Carmen tried to describe the summer festival. She wanted to share the sights and sounds with Ling the best she could.

5   The Renaissance Festival is set up to be like a country village in England in the late 1500s. The villagers wear bright costumes made of cotton, silk, and velvet. Visitors can rent costumes, too.

6   Knights in armor battle on horseback. There are targets for practicing with a bow and arrow. Some people try their skill at fencing with swords.

7   A wooden stage is built in the shade of trees. That is the place where actors perform. They do magic shows and puppet shows. Musicians also play there for people who dance on stilts. The dancers wear long, colorful fringed pants over the tall, wooden stilts. The pants make the stilts look like long legs. The audience applauds as the dancers move on the stage in time with the music.

8   There is always a play going on somewhere at the festival. Actors in costume walk around the festival carrying their props in a trunk. Visitors are asked to join in a play. They can also shout and sing as part of the audience. Carmen said it was certainly different from any other play she had seen!

9   Carmen told Ling that when she was there she had been picked for one of the plays. She played a good princess with a heart of gold. During the play, she had to fight a fire-breathing dragon!

10   "Fighting the dragon was easy! Keeping the pointed hat on my head and the veil of the hat out of my mouth was the hard part," Carmen explained. "The audience laughed, but no one laughed more than I did."

11   Carmen waited for Ling to comment on her idea. Finally, Ling told Carmen the idea sounded just right for the show.

12   "My idea is just right for *Just for Openers,*" thought Carmen, "and so am I."

Knowing the Words

Write the words from the story that have the meanings below.

1. sport using thin swords _____
   (Par. 6)

2. trimmed with threads _____
   (Par. 7)

3. thin cloth for
   covering the face _____
   (Par. 10)

Check the meaning of the underlined word in each sentence.

4. The actors walked through the crowd carrying a <u>trunk</u> full of props.

   ____ the main part of something

   ____ a large box with a lid

5. The musicians will <u>play</u> for the dancers.

   ____ make an instrument work

   ____ actions done for fun

Learning to Study

This chart tells about the events at the festival for two days. Use the chart to answer the questions.

EVENTS	SATURDAY	SUNDAY
Puppet show	2:00 and 4:00	2:00 and 4:00
Dancing	3:00 only	3:00 and 5:00
Fencing	1:00 and 3:00	1:00 only
Plays	2:00 and 4:00	2:00 and 4:00

1. What two events begin at the same time both days? _____

2. On what day is dancing scheduled only one time? _____

3. What could you see at 4:00 on Sunday if you didn't want to see a play?

   _____

Reading and Thinking

Write **T** before the sentences that are true. Write **F** before the sentences that are false.

1. ____ Carmen gave Ling an idea for a show.

2. ____ Carmen wore a hat.

3. ____ Carmen rode on horseback.

4. ____ The festival has a puppet show.

Write **E** before each group of words that describe events in an English village in the 1500s. Write **C** before each group of words that describe modern events.

5. ____ knights riding horses

6. ____ people driving cars

7. ____ dancers on stilts

8. ____ villagers using bows and arrows

9. Check the reason the author probably wrote this story.

   ____ to tell about Carmen in a play

   ____ to tell about a special festival

   ____ to tell about old-fashioned clothes

10. Do you think Carmen will share other ideas for the show? Why or why not?

    _____

Working with Words

Check the correct meaning of the underlined word.

1. He watched the play in <u>amazement</u>.

   ____ the act of being amazed

   ____ not amazed

   ____ amazed before

2. She was <u>speechless</u> during the show.

   ____ before speech

   ____ act of speech

   ____ without speech

Heads Above the Rest

Why do you think the artist chose these four people ?

1 It was late in the afternoon. Ling and the cast had just finished watching tapes for Saturday's show. Some of the cast members had already left. Others were still gathering their things to go. Kim bent over to pick up her backpack. In seconds its contents were scattered across the floor. The bottom of the backpack had ripped.

2 Kim looked disgusted, but Laurie and Ben just smiled. They all started to pick the things up from the floor.

3 "What's this?" Laurie asked, showing something to Kim.

4 "It's supposed to be an eagle. I tried to carve it out of soapstone. The beak was the hardest part. I never thought carving something could be so tricky," said Kim, taking the eagle from Laurie.

5 "I've never tried to carve anything," Ben said. "I imagine it's hard."

6 "While you're imagining, Ben, think about the man who carved Mount Rushmore," said Kim. "I thought of that when I was carving this eagle. I don't know *how* that was done."

7 "My art teacher once told us about the artist who carved Mount Rushmore," said Laurie. "The man who designed the heads was Gutzon Borglum. The heads of the four presidents are each sixty feet tall. If those heads were attached to bodies, each figure would be four hundred sixty-five feet tall!"

8 "It must have been hard to carve something so large," Kim said.

9 "There weren't any roads to the mountain. The workers had to ride horses or walk to the job. Then they had to climb for half an hour to get to the top of the mountain. To do their job, the workers were lowered from the top of the mountain in harnesses," Laurie told them.

10 "I'd be tired before I ever started to work," said Ben. "Did they just chip away at the stone to carve the heads?"

11 "No. My teacher said they used dynamite. They would blast away the cracked rock on the surface of the mountain. Then they could carve into the solid rock underneath," Laurie explained. "If a head was carved in cracked rock, water might get into the cracks and freeze. Then part of the head—the nose, for example—might break off!"

12 They all laughed as they pictured a big nose falling from the mountain.

13 "Borglum wanted the monument to be perfect. It took over fourteen years to finish the project," Laurie added.

14 "I know how long I worked on my eagle," sighed Kim. "I'll leave the mountains to someone else."

Photograph by Paul Brown

Knowing the Words

Write the words from the story that have the meanings below.

1. upset _____
   (Par. 2)

2. leather straps used to
   hold something or someone _____
   (Par. 9)

3. an explosive _____
   (Par. 11)

Check the meaning of the homograph as it is used in each sentence.

4. Mom will <u>leave</u> your presents with me.
   ____ allow to remain behind
   ____ have permission to go

5. I <u>long</u> to see my friends who have moved.
   ____ having greater length than usual
   ____ wish for something

Learning to Study

1. Complete the following outline. Use paragraph 9 to complete Part I. Use paragraph 11 to complete Part II.

   I. Problems of getting to work

      A. _____

      B. _____
         _____

   II. Problems with cracked rock

      A. _____

      B. _____

Write these dictionary entry words in syllables to show where the words can be divided at the end of a line of writing.

2. scatter _____

3. suppose _____

4. surface _____

Reading and Thinking

1. Check the sentence that best states the main idea of the story.
   ____ Gutzon Borglum is a famous artist.
   ____ Carving Mount Rushmore was difficult.
   ____ Carving an eagle is difficult.

Write **T** before the sentences that are true.
Write **F** before the sentences that are false.

2. ____ The heads of four presidents are carved into Mount Rushmore.

3. ____ Mount Rushmore was finished in ten years.

4. ____ Some workers walked to their jobs.

5. What might happen if the carving was not done in solid rock? _____
   _____

Circle the word that best completes each sentence.

6. The ____ of the box were counted.
   designs   contents   artists

7. The artist carved a ____ piece of wood.
   solid   tired   disgusted

Working with Words

Check the correct meaning of the underlined word.

1. The tape was <u>useless</u> once it got tangled.
   ____ used
   ____ without use
   ____ used before

2. Each child was given a <u>lovable</u> puppy.
   ____ loved after
   ____ without love
   ____ can be loved

Natural Artist

Could you draw a picture without using your hands?

1 Kim and Laurie stood outside the studio waiting for their ride home. Laurie's dad was picking them up after the meeting for the show. He'd be there in a few minutes.

2 Kim and Laurie moved away from the entrance of the building. A crowd of people hurried by them as Laurie turned to Kim. "I think I'd be able to spot you easily in a large group of people, Kim," she said, smiling. "Since the first day I met you, I can't remember seeing you without that bright red backpack on your shoulders."

3 Kim laughed. "I have to get a new one. The bottom is torn on this one, but I've had it for a long time. I didn't realize that I always have a backpack with me. I decided to use it when I saw my teacher carry one to school every day," she explained. "She told me that a friend of hers always used a backpack, but he did it for a different reason."

4 "Now I'm curious," said Laurie. "What was his reason?"

5 "His name is Daniel," said Kim. "He is an artist, but he doesn't have any arms. He's attending an art college here in Chicago. That's where my teacher met him. They were in the same drawing class. One day my teacher was walking to class. Her arms were filled with books. She reached the door of the building and was struggling to get it open when someone opened it for her. It was Daniel! His own supplies were in a backpack. He stood on one foot and opened the door with the other one. After that, she got a backpack, too."

6 "Is that why you always carry one, Kim?" asked Laurie with a smile.

7 "I'm always looking for good ideas," Kim said. "I took Daniel's good idea, but I can't take his talent. He is determined to be the best artist he can be."

8 "How does he draw or paint?" Laurie asked.

9 "He grasps the brush or pencil in his toes," answered Kim. "When Daniel was growing up, he learned to use his feet the way we use our hands. It was natural for him. He didn't know feet weren't supposed to work like hands."

10 "Do you think he'll become famous?" Laurie asked.

11 "He might," Kim said. "If he does, it will not be as a person with a disability who paints with his feet. He'll be famous for his talent as an artist."

Knowing the Words

Write the words from the story that have the meanings below.

1. eager to know _____
   (Par. 4)
2. trying with great effort _____
   (Par. 5)
3. holds _____
   (Par. 9)

A **synonym** is a word with the same or nearly the same meaning as another word. Circle each pair of synonyms below.

4. group—crowd
5. struggle—easy
6. friend—enemy
7. natural—awkward
8. hurried—rushed
9. smile—grin

Learning to Study

Use the want ad below to answer the questions.

> § Paintings Wanted §
> For Personal Collection
> Paying top dollar
> American artists only
> Call M. Hill at 555-0011

1. Will M. Hill buy or sell paintings?
   _____

2. Why does M. Hill want paintings?
   _____

3. What kind of artists' paintings are wanted? _____

Next to each artist's name below, write the encyclopedia letter you would use to find facts about the artist.

4. ____ Frederic Remington
5. ____ Mary Cassatt
6. ____ Norman Rockwell
7. ____ Georgia O'Keeffe

Reading and Thinking

1. What does Kim always carry?
   _____

2. How does Daniel hold his paintbrush?
   _____

3. Why is Daniel so good at using his feet to draw and paint? _____
   _____

4. Do you think Daniel would be a good classmate? Why or why not? _____
   _____

5. Write the name of the character these words describe.

   polite   talented   determined
   _____

Working with Words

Check the correct meaning of the underlined word.

1. If you are a <u>nonswimmer</u> you must stay in the shallow end of the pool.
   ____ act of swimming
   ____ not a swimmer
   ____ able to swim

2. He gave the teacher a <u>reasonable</u> answer.
   ____ full of reasons
   ____ opposite of reason
   ____ capable of having reason

3. The <u>homeless</u> dog was wet and cold.
   ____ without a home
   ____ before a home
   ____ not home

Behind the Scenes

Do TV viewers always see what really happens on a program?

1   "Ben, do you remember before you were on the show? We asked viewers to send us ideas for programs," Ling said. "You sent in your suggestion for a raft trip down the Mississippi River."

2   Ben smiled and nodded. "I think of that each time I read a suggestion letter from one of the viewers. I remember watching the show at home. I was so happy you had used my idea! You talked with a man named Glen. He was floating down the Mississippi on a raft he had built."

3   "That's right," said Ling. "Did I ever tell you what happened while we were taping it?"

4   Ben shook his head.

5   "As I recall," Ling said, "Glen had made a raft by attaching an old house trailer to a wooden platform. He started down the river at Minneapolis, Minnesota. We arranged to meet him at a small river town in Iowa, but the crew and I almost ended his trip there!"

6   Ben looked puzzled. "I didn't see anything wrong when I watched the show."

7   Ling laughed. "What you didn't see was all of us falling into the river! When James, Nancy, and I jumped on board, the whole raft tipped!"

8   "Was anyone hurt?" Ben asked.

9   "We were all wearing life jackets, so we just got wet," Ling said, smiling. "James even managed to hold on to his camera. Things happened so quickly, though, no one could grab Glen's motor in time."

10   "It sank?" Ben asked.

11   "To the bottom!" Ling answered. "Glen was really upset because he couldn't afford to buy a new one. Without the motor, his trip might have taken a year instead of the five months he had planned."

12   "What a situation," Ben remarked.

13   "What saved the trip was Glen's friendliness," Ling said. "The people in that Iowa town really liked him. When his motor sank, they helped him buy a new one. The crew and I helped, too."

14   "Wasn't there also something about trees in that show?" asked Ben.

15   "You have a very good memory, Ben," Ling said. "We called that the 'chain' of trees. The people in every town where Glen stopped gave him a tree. He would plant that tree in the following town. Then *those* people would give him a tree to take along to the next town. By the end of the trip, Glen had planted fifty trees along the river."

16   "After listening to your story, Ling," Ben said, laughing, "it sounds as if my idea was all wet!"

Knowing the Words

Write the words from the story that have the meanings below.

1. type of moveable home _____
(Par. 5)

2. certain condition _____
(Par. 12)

Match the word in the first column with its abbreviation.

3. ____ Mississippi   **a.** IA

4. ____ Minnesota   **b.** MS

5. ____ Iowa   **c.** MN

6. An **idiom** is a group of words that has a special meaning. Write the idiom in paragraph 16.

_____

Learning to Study

1. Complete the following outline. Use the facts in paragraph 5 to complete Part I. Use the facts in paragraphs 7–11 to complete Part II.

   I. Glen prepares for trip

     A. _____

     B. _____

     C. _____

   II.   River accident

     A. _____

     B. _____

     C. _____

2. Number the words below in alphabetical order.

____ drill   ____ control

____ doubt   ____ drift

____ dried   ____ date

Reading and Thinking

1. Check the sentence that best states the main idea of the story.

____ Ling goes on a trip.

____ Ling helps plant trees.

____ Ling describes taping a show.

Circle the word that correctly completes each sentence.

2. The girls played on the ____ in the pool at the apartment.

     river   raft   motor

3. I can ____ to buy a present for my friend's birthday.

     attach   afford   memory

Write **T** before the sentences that are true. Write **F** before the sentences that are false.

4. ____ The trip started in Iowa.

5. ____ The raft tipped over.

6. ____ The crew's camera sank.

7. ____ The townspeople helped Glen buy a new motor.

8. ____ Glen planted trees along the way.

9. Write a summary for paragraph 13. Include the points given below.

   Glen's friendliness   people's help

_____

_____

Working with Words

Write **S** if the possessive word is singular. Write **P** if the possessive word is plural.

1. ____ pencil's   **5.** ____ people's

2. ____ trees'   **6.** ____ camera's

3. ____ raft's   **7.** ____ jackets'

4. ____ programs'   **8.** ____ river's

Baseball Dreams

Do you have a sports hero?

1 "This is going to be a dream come true," Kate said to her family. They were on their way to Cooperstown, New York, the home of the Baseball Hall of Fame.

2 "We know how much you like baseball, Kate," said her mom. "At the first sign of spring, you're out on the diamond hitting balls and catching grounders."

3 "I'm just a baseball machine," said Kate, laughing. "Are we almost there?"

4 "Be patient, Kate. The Hall of Fame has been here in Cooperstown since 1939, and it's not going to disappear today," said her dad.

5 When they arrived, Mr. Wilkins parked the car. Kate and Ben raced ahead to the entrance. "Ben, will you help me find Ernie Banks in the Hall of Fame?" Kate asked.

6 "Of course, Kate," Ben said to his sister. Ben had heard Kate talk about Ernie Banks before. Ernie played for the Chicago Cubs for nineteen years. He was twice voted Most Valuable Player in the National League. Ernie Banks was Kate's favorite baseball player of all time.

7 "Kate, do you know how players get into the Hall of Fame?" Ben asked as they searched for Ernie's picture.

8 "Yes, I do. I've read all about it," Kate said proudly. "The players are elected by sportswriters and a special committee. Usually a player has to be retired for five years before he can be elected. And he has to have played for at least ten years."

9 "You do know a lot, Kate," said Ben. "How many players would you guess are in the Hall of Fame?"

10 "I don't know the exact number, but I think there are about two hundred. If you don't believe me, you could always count them yourself," answered Kate.

11 "I believe you. I believe you," Ben said, laughing.

12 Suddenly Kate grew quiet. "Look!" she said in a hushed voice. "Here he is, Ben. Here's Ernie Banks."

13 The two children gazed at the gleaming bronze likeness of Ernie Banks. Then they read the words below describing Ernie's outstanding achievements. Kate sighed happily as she stared into her hero's eyes. She seemed to be in another world.

14 Ben and his parents began to examine the bats, balls, gloves, and uniforms displayed nearby. Each object once belonged to a famous player. A card beside each piece of equipment gave its history.

15 At last it was time to leave. Ben had to give Kate a little shake to wake her from her dream come true.

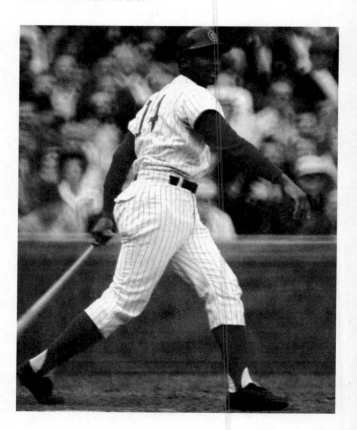

Knowing the Words

Write the words from the story that have the meanings below.

1. made of copper and tin _____
(Par. 13)

2. something having a similar appearance _____
(Par. 13)

3. the acts of reaching a goal; successes _____
(Par. 13)

4. shown _____
(Par. 14)

Check the meaning of the underlined word in each sentence.

5. The <u>diamond</u> sparkled in the light.

_____ infield in baseball

_____ jewel

6. The doctor said the <u>patient</u> was well.

_____ willing to wait

_____ person treated by a doctor

7. The worker <u>retired</u> after twenty years.

_____ went to bed

_____ stopped working

Learning to Study

Use the entry below to answer the questions.

bank /bangk/ *n* **1** place of business for handling money **2** the land around a river

1. Underline the sentence in which *bank* has the same meaning as the first definition.

Kate sat on the bank of the river.

The sports star put his savings in the bank.

2. Write a sentence that uses *bank* meaning "the land around a river."

_____

Reading and Thinking

Circle the word that best completes each sentence.

1. The _____ was made into a ring for Kay's birthday.

shoe   diamond   vest

2. The doctor had to _____ the child.

build   sing   examine

3. Check the reason the author probably wrote this story.

_____ to tell the history of baseball

_____ to tell about the Chicago Cubs

_____ to tell about Kate's sports hero

4. Write a sentence from the story that tells how anxious Kate is for baseball season to start.

_____

_____

_____

5. Do you think Kate will continue to play baseball after her visit to New York? Why or why not?

_____

_____

Working with Words

Fill in each blank with the possessive form of the word in parentheses.

1. West View is the _____ favorite park. (people)

2. The woman needed the _____ wool to make the yarn. (sheep)

3. Brushing brightens the _____ shine. (teeth)

The Bears of Yellowstone

Why were the bears of Yellowstone a problem?

1 "Will we see any bears in Yellowstone National Park, Mom?" Kate asked as her father drove the car into the park.

2 Mrs. Wilkins smiled at her daughter. "Are you hoping we will or hoping we won't?"

3 "I'm not sure," Kate admitted. "I know the park used to have bears that would come up to the cars of the visitors. I don't think I want to be *that* close to one."

4 "We'll ask my friend, Bill Freeman," her father said. "He's been a ranger for the park since we both graduated from college. He'll be able to answer your question."

5 Since the last day of the school year, Ben and Kate had been counting the days until this trip. The family had flown to Wyoming. Then they had rented a car so they could drive through Yellowstone and see all the sights.

6 "Will Mr. Freeman have his daughter and son with him?" asked Ben.

7 His father nodded. "They're about your ages. Mr. Freeman says that Eddie and Robyn know the park almost as well as he does. They'll show us around while he's on duty."

8 Soon they reached the Visitors Center. Mr. Freeman and his children were already there. Kate waited for her father to introduce the family, and then she asked her question. "Are there bears here?" she asked Mr. Freeman.

9 "Yes, there are bears here, Kate, but you probably won't see them."

10 "Why not?" Kate asked, looking around.

11 "Years ago you would have seen bears all around. They begged for food and raided garbage cans near the hotels and shops," Mr. Freeman told her. "As many as forty people were hurt by the bears each year. In 1967 we started a plan to keep the bears in the woods where they belong."

12 "How did you do that?" asked Ben. "The park is too big to fence them in."

13 "You're right, Ben. We closed the garbage areas and asked tourists not to feed the bears. When some bears still kept coming into the tourist areas, we caught them and took them to wilder parts of the park. This plan took about ten years, but it worked," said Mr. Freeman. "Today Yellowstone has more bears than ever, but they stay in the back country."

14 "Yellowstone is known for other things besides bears," said Robyn. "Old Faithful is famous, and there are bubbling mudpots, a mountain of glass, and trees of stone. And, of course, there are the yellow stones that give the park its name."

15 "I can't *bear* to wait a minute longer," said Ben, laughing. "Let's see Yellowstone!"

Photograph by Johnny Johnson

Knowing the Words

Write the words from the story that have the meanings below.

1. a guard or
   keeper of a park _____
   (Par. 4)

2. attacked and
   took something _____
   (Par. 11)

Underline the word with the correct meaning in each sentence below.

3. Kate ____ like to see the mudpot in the park. (would, wood)

4. Each rope on the tent had a ____ at the end. (knot, not)

A **synonym** is a word with the same or nearly the same meaning as another word. Write the pair of synonyms from each sentence.

5. He was on duty because no one else could do his job that day.

   _____

6. The shops were filled with people who enjoyed looking through the stores.

   _____

Learning to Study

Write the letter you would look under to find facts in the encyclopedia to answer each of the questions below.

1. What does a ranger do? _____

2. How large is Yellowstone Park? _____

3. What is Old Faithful? _____

4. What main topic could you look under to find facts in the encyclopedia that would answer questions 2 and 3?

   _____

Reading and Thinking

1. Check the reason the author probably wrote this story.

   ____ to tell about a ranger

   ____ to tell about bears at Yellowstone

   ____ to tell about camping in Yellowstone

Circle the word that best completes each sentence.

2. Ben's dad was ____ on Mr. Freeman to show them the park.

   begging   counting   looking

3. We ____ to see her this week.

   plan   reach   show

Write **Y** before the words that describe the bears in Yellowstone Park today. Write **B** before the words that describe the bears in Yellowstone Park before 1967.

4. ____ stay in back country

5. ____ more bears than ever before

6. ____ raid garbage cans near hotels and shops

7. ____ come up to cars of the visitors

8. Write a summary for paragraph 11. Include the points given below.

   bears as a problem   plan for the bears

   _____

   _____

Working with Words

Fill in each blank with the possessive form of the word in parentheses.

1. The _____ cars had green tags while in the park. (visitors)

2. The _____ owner liked working with the tourists. (shop)

79

The Wonders of Yellowstone

Which of Yellowstone's wonders would you like best?

1 Ben shook his head as he walked toward Old Faithful. "Yellowstone is so strange," he said to his mom. "Steam shoots out of the ground, and some of the lakes are hot. Eddie told me about some trees that have turned to stone. Most of the rocks I see are yellow. Why is everything so different here?"

2 "Millions of years ago volcanoes exploded again and again in this area," Mrs. Wilkins explained. "Lava from them flowed over this land and left these rocks yellow."

3 "That's right," Robyn said. "There's still hot, melted rock underground. It heats the rainwater that seeps down there. Some of the hot water comes to the surface slowly as hot springs. Some is heated until it turns into steam. Pressure builds up. Then steam explodes as a geyser."

4 As they approached Old Faithful, steam suddenly shot high into the air. Ben and the other tourists gasped in amazement. "You just witnessed Yellowstone's most famous geyser in action. About every seventy-seven minutes, Old Faithful shoots boiling water more than one hundred feet into the air," Robyn explained.

5 "Let's go see the mudpots," Eddie said. "They're another wonder of Yellowstone."

6 Kate was surprised when she saw the sea of mud. The mudpots are caused by steam and gas rising. Kate saw bubbles in shades of brown, pink, and yellow. They were forming on the surface of the mud. Some were as big as basketballs. "That's colored mud!" Kate exclaimed.

7 "The colors come from minerals in the mud," Eddie explained. "The mudpots are my favorite things in the park."

8 Finally, the rest of the group persuaded Kate and Robyn to leave the mudpots and go to see the "stone" trees. On the way, they drove past black cliffs that sparkled in the sun. From a distance the cliffs look like black glass. They were formed from hot lava that had cooled quickly. The black rock was so hard that Native Americans once used it to make arrowheads.

9 As they neared the stone trees, Ben asked, "Where are the leaves?" Only tree stumps remained, and they had turned to stone.

10 Eddie smiled and explained, "The leaves burned thousands of years ago when ash and mud from the volcanoes buried these trees. The trees slowly began turning to stone. Even today you can see the rings on some of the stumps. The number of rings is the same as the number of years the tree lived."

11 Kate turned to Ben. "If you were a tree, Ben, you'd have more rings than I would," Kate said jokingly.

Photograph by Frank S. Balthis

Knowing the Words

Write the words from the story that have the meanings below.

1. leaks _____
   (Par. 3)

2. a spring shooting
   steam into the air _____
   (Par. 3)

3. saw for yourself _____
   (Par. 4)

4. solid material dug
   from the earth _____
   (Par. 7)

A **synonym** is a word with the same or nearly the same meaning as another word. Write the words from the story that are synonyms for these words.

5. stone _____
   (Par. 3)

6. warmed _____
   (Par. 3)

7. climbing _____
   (Par. 6)

Learning to Study

Read the graph and answer the questions.

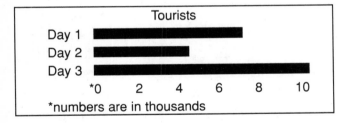

Tourists

Day 1
Day 2
Day 3
*0   2   4   6   8   10
*numbers are in thousands

1. What day had the largest number of

   tourists? _____

2. What day had fewer than six thousand

   tourists? _____

Syllables show where words can be divided at the end of a line of writing. Use a dictionary to write these words in syllables.

3. volcano _____

4. arrowheads _____

Reading and Thinking

1. Check the sentence that best states the main idea of this story.

   ____ Volcanoes can change the land.

   ____ Tourists come to enjoy the park.

   ____ Yellowstone has interesting sights.

2. What is Old Faithful? _____

3. What gives the mudpots their colors?

   _____

4. What did Native Americans make out of

   hard rock? _____

5. What caused the rock in Yellowstone to

   be yellow? _____

   _____

6. Why are Robyn and Eddie good guides

   for the Wilkins family? _____

   _____

   _____

Working with Words

Write a compound word using two words in each sentence.

1. Balls thrown into baskets are

   _____.

2. An area of ground used as a place to

   camp is a _____.

3. A place under the surface of the ground

   is _____.

4. Wood used to burn in a fire is

   _____.

The Ghost of the Prairie

Do you like to hear ghost stories?

1   On Friday, Mr. Freeman took the Wilkins family and his own children on a backpacking trip. He had the necessary camping and fishing permits so the two families could hike far into Yellowstone. At dinner time they stopped for the night at a clearing on the bank of a beautiful lake. Ben helped his dad pitch the tents Mr. Freeman had brought.

2   Mrs. Wilkins carefully started a fire in a spot away from trees and bushes. Eddie began peeling potatoes. Mr. Freeman, Kate, and Robyn stood at the edge of the lake. They were trying to catch what they would eat for dinner.

3   The children had good luck fishing. Everyone sat around the campfire and ate the delicious catch that Mr. Wilkins had fried.

4   "Sitting around a campfire makes me want to hear a good ghost story," said Robyn.

5   Mr. Freeman winked at his children. "Would you like to hear about the Laramie Ghost?"

6   "Let me tell about the ghost," Eddie said. He had heard this story before.

7   "Back in 1870," he began, "a soldier named Lieutenant Allison was stationed at Fort Laramie, Wyoming. One day he rode alone across the prairie.

8   "Suddenly, he heard *two* sets of hoofbeats. In the distance, Allison saw a woman. She was dressed in green, and she rode a black horse.

9   "The lieutenant decided to follow her. He had almost caught up with her when the horse and its rider disappeared over a low hill. Allison rode to the top of the hill. He saw nothing. The horse and rider had vanished!

10   "When Allison came back to the fort," Eddie went on, "he told what had happened. An old-timer explained that the rider he had seen was the Laramie Ghost. The ghost had been the daughter of one of the fort's first settlers. She rode away from the fort one day, about forty years before, and she never returned. On the day she left the fort, she was dressed in green, and the horse she was riding was as black as night.

11   "Lieutenant Allison gasped. Had he seen the Laramie Ghost?"

12   "The story doesn't end there," said Mr. Freeman. "People say the settler's daughter returns to ride across the prairie every seven years!"

13   Suddenly leaves rustled in the darkness. The campers heard something scamper away. Kate jumped up and knocked Ben over.

14   "Don't worry, Kate," said Robyn. "This isn't the year for the Laramie Ghost to ride."

Knowing the Words

Write the words from the story that have the meanings below.

1. walk a long distance _____
   (Par. 1)

2. given a duty _____
   (Par. 7)

Underline the word with the correct meaning in each sentence below.

3. It took ____ hours to set up camp. (four, for)

4. Kate ____ strange sounds coming from the woods. (herd, heard)

5. Eddie was the ____ to tell the strange ghost story. (won, one)

6. Write the simile found in paragraph 10.

   _____

Learning to Study

This map shows Ft. Laramie and part of the Oregon Trail. Use the map to answer the questions below.

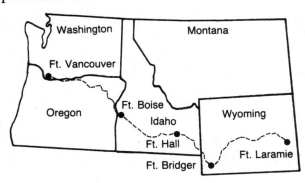

1. How many states are shown? _____

2. In what state is Ft. Laramie? _____

3. How many states on the map did this part of the Oregon Trail cross? _____

4. What two forts are in Idaho? _____

Reading and Thinking

Circle the word that best completes each sentence.

1. We ____ a tent in a clearing.
   followed   decided   pitched

2. The ranger has to ____ the wild bird.
   catch   vanish   rustle

3. Do you think Ben will tell the story of the Laramie Ghost to his friends? Why or why not? _____

   _____

4. Why didn't the lieutenant catch up to the woman on the black horse?

   _____

Write **T** before the sentences that are true. Write **F** before the sentences that are false.

5. ____ The woman left the fort this year.

6. ____ Allison was the son of a settler.

7. ____ The woman rode out of the fort.

8. Write a summary for paragraph 9. Include the points given below.

   Allison's try   rider's disappearance

   _____

   _____

Working with Words

Write a compound word using two words in each sentence.

1. The beat from the hoof of a horse is a

   _____.

2. A pack worn on your back is a

   _____.

A New Year

How do you feel when something begins again?

1   "This fire is really hot!" Mr. Wilkins said. He was cooking hamburgers on the grill in the backyard while Kate watched.

2   "Maybe we need a robot that can cook," Kate suggested to her dad. "It wouldn't be bothered by the heat."

3   Ben was putting plates and cups on the picnic table. "I remember when you wanted a robot to clean our rooms," he said. "It's too bad robots can't think. I could use some extra brainpower to think of some good ideas. Our first meeting to plan shows for next year is only two weeks away."

4   "One of my friends went to a big rodeo in Houston last year," offered Kate. "Could you go there and take me?"

5   Ben smiled. "I'll suggest it at the meeting. Thanks for the idea, Kate."

6   Mrs. Wilkins brought out a bowl of fruit for their picnic. "A nurse at work had an unusual vacation last year. She and her family worked on a farm in Ontario, Canada," Mrs. Wilkins said. "That would be an unusual experience for city people."

7   "Don't forget we're all going to Florida next summer to visit our friends, the Smiths," said Dad. "Your mom has part of the trip planned already. We can try snorkeling, and we'll go to Disney World."

8   *"All right!"* shouted Kate. "I'll get my suntan lotion and sunglasses right now."

9   "Those are all great ideas for the show. You gave me the extra brainpower I needed," Ben said, smiling. "I remember some ideas the cast members gave Ling during the year. Kim mentioned going to New Mexico for a hot air balloon festival, and Laurie had a good idea about lighthouses."

10   "Your viewers might like to see the dripstones in Mammoth Cave," Ben's dad said. "Right now, though, the only thing that is *dripping* is the juice from the hamburgers. Come and get it!"

11   They all sat around the picnic table. "I'm really lucky to be on TV doing 'Ben, the Traveler'," said Ben.

12   "You're not on the show because you're lucky," said his mom. "You're on the show because you had confidence in yourself and in your ideas."

13   "Having confidence in your ideas can make dreams come true," said Ben. "I learned that from the people I met this year. You're right, Mom. Dreams and good ideas do run in this family."

Knowing the Words

Write the words from the story that have the meanings below.

1. a show of skill
   with horses and cattle _____
   (Par. 4)

2. trust _____
   (Par. 12)

Check the meaning of the underlined word in each sentence.

3. Rose wanted to <u>bowl</u> on Thursday nights, but the league was closed.

   ____ a dish with high sides

   ____ play a game by rolling a ball

4. He turned <u>right</u> at the corner.

   ____ correct

   ____ a direction

Learning to Study

Read this recipe Ben might follow when he cooks. Then answer the questions.

Pancakes	
1 cup flour	1 cup milk
2 teaspoons baking powder	1 egg
2 tablespoons sugar	3 tablespoons butter (melted)
1/4 teaspoon salt	

Mix flour, baking powder, sugar, and salt in medium bowl. Beat egg, add milk and butter, beat again. Pour into bowl with flour mixture and stir till lumpy. Pour 1/4 cup batter into hot pan for each pancake. Cook till bubbles form on top. Turn and cook 2 minutes longer.

1. Write the items that are mixed with the flour.

   _____

2. How much batter is needed for each pancake?

   _____

3. What kind of butter is used? _____

Reading and Thinking

Write **F** before the sentences that are facts. Write **O** before the sentences that are opinions.

1. ____ Robots aren't bothered by heat.

2. ____ Summer vacations are boring.

3. ____ A rodeo is held in Houston.

4. ____ Mammoth Cave is fun to visit.

5. ____ People go snorkeling in Florida.

6. Check the sentence that best states the main idea of the story.

   ____ The family shares ideas for the new season of Ben's show.

   ____ The Wilkins family has a picnic.

   ____ The family plans a trip to Florida.

7. Why does Ben need ideas for the show?

   _____

8. Does Ben trust himself? Why or why not? _____

   _____

Working with Words

Write a compound word using two words in each sentence.

1. Water that has salt in it is

   _____.

2. A book used for taking notes is a

   _____.

3. A person who makes sales is a

   _____.

4. A cloth that covers a table is a

   _____.

Checking Understanding

1. The event takes place in

   _____.

2. Check the reason the event is called the Changing of the Guard.

   _____ Both soldiers change directions.

   _____ The two soldiers are called guards.

   _____ One guard replaces another guard.

3. What does the officer do?

   _____

4. Underline two sentences that are true. (2)

   Tourists see the Changing of the Guard.

   The buried soldiers are unknown.

   The guards talk to each other.

   Tourists take part in the ceremony.

5. The soldier guarding the tomb is a part

   of an _____.

6. Check the main idea of the story.

   _____ Touring Washington, D.C., is fun.

   _____ Honor guards are soldiers.

   _____ The Changing of the Guard is a special ceremony.

7. Check two actions both soldiers do during the ceremony (2)

   _____ change rifles   _____ tap heels

   _____ pace   _____ salute

8. What does an honor guard need to be able to do?

   _____ march to music

   _____ know the cemetery history

   _____ name the soldiers buried in the Tomb of the Unknowns

Number of Words
Read per Minute [ ]

Test Score
(Possible Score—10) [ ]

---

1. Where did Laurie live when she became interested in lighthouses?

   _____

2. Check what was used to build the first Boston Light.

   _____ steel _____ wood _____ bricks

3. Check the two things that often caused lighthouses to be destroyed. (2)

   _____ fire _____ storms _____ rocks

4. What do modern lighthouses look like?

   _____

5. What now runs some modern

   lighthouses? _____

6. Why is steel used to build new

   lighthouses? _____

   _____

7. Who rescued sailors? _____

8. Check two sentences that are true. (2)

   _____ Lighthouses have changed.

   _____ Boston Light is on an island.

   _____ Today, lighthouses use fire for light.

   _____ Lighthouses always help ships.

Number of Words
Read per Minute [ ]

Test Score
(Possible Score—10) [ ]

Checking Understanding

1. Mount St. Helens is in what state?

   _____

2. Check the sentence that is true.

   ____ The volcano in Mount St. Helens exploded in 1980.

   ____ Lava flowed out of Mount St. Helens.

   ____ Nothing can live on Mount St. Helens.

3. Why does Carmen's brother know so much about volcanoes and earthquakes?

   _____

4. Why was Joe at Mount St. Helen's when it exploded? _____

5. What caused the ice on the mountain to melt? _____

6. The fish in the nearest river were destroyed because _____

   _____.

7. Check three signs of life on the mountain. (3)

   ____ flowers   ____ melted rock

   ____ lava   ____ ferns

   ____ ash   ____ deer tracks

8. Ash fell in towns as far away as

   _____.

Number of Words Read per Minute [ ]

Test Score (Possible Score—10) [ ]

1. Check the main idea of the story.

   ____ camping accidents

   ____ trip to Wyoming

   ____ bears in a national park

2. Mr. Freeman knows about Yellowstone Park because _____.

3. Write the three actions taken to protect tourists against the bears. (3)

   _____

   _____

   _____

4. How long did it take to rid the tourist areas of bears? _____

5. Why were bears found around the hotels?

   _____

6. Check one reason fences weren't used to control the bears.

   ____ harmful to bears

   ____ size of park

   ____ materials not available

7. Why were bears kept in the woods?

   _____

8. Check the sentence that is true.

   ____ Yellowstone has more bears now than ever.

   ____ Bears have left Yellowstone Park.

   ____ All park hotels are closed.

Number of Words Read per Minute [ ]

Test Score (Possible Score—10) [ ]

Knowing the Words

Write the words from the story that have the meanings below.

1. someone in charge of a show ___producer___ (Par. 2)
2. adjusted to make clearer ___focused___ (Par. 3)
3. a particular place ___location___ (Par. 6)
4. a level of school after high school ___college___ (Par. 6)
5. special assignments ___projects___ (Par. 6)

A **synonym** is a word with the same or nearly the same meaning as another word. Circle each pair of synonyms.

6. location—vacation
7. (finish—complete)
8. blink—stare
9. (bumped—hit)

Learning to Study

Number the words in each column in alphabetical order.

1. _3_ program
   _1_ prepare
   _2_ producer
2. _1_ interview
   _2_ introduce
   _3_ invited

Guide words are printed at the top of most pages in a dictionary. The guide word at the left is the first word on the page. The guide word at the right is the last word on the page. Check each word that could be found on a page having the guide words shown in dark print.

3. **brand—brim**
   ___ brake ___ broken ✓ break
4. **fast—favor**
   ___ family ✓ father ___ fame
5. **home—hope**
   ___ host ✓ honest ___ hotel

Reading and Thinking

Write **T** before the sentences that are true. Write **F** before the sentences that are false.

1. _T_ Ben has been on vacation.
2. _T_ Ben is a cast member on a program for children.
3. _F_ Ben has never worked on the show.
4. _F_ Ben does the science reports on the program.
5. _T_ Ling is the producer of the show.
6. Check the sentence that best states the main idea of the story.
   ___ Ben tells the cast and crew about his summer vacation.
   ___ Ben shares his ideas for the show with Ling.
   ✓ Ben and the cast start a new year working on the show.
7. Why did Ben go to Michigan last year?
   He did a show about the National
   Music Camp. (Answers may vary.)

Working with Words

A **prefix** is a group of letters added to the beginning of a word to change its meaning. The prefix **pre-** means "before." For example, *preview* means "to view before." Add **pre-** to each word below. Use each new word in a sentence.

1. _pre_ pay _____
   (Sentences will vary.)
2. _pre_ heat _____
   (Sentences will vary.)
3. _pre_ package _____
   (Sentences will vary.)

3

Knowing the Words

Write the words from the story that have the meanings below.

1. talking about ___discussing___ (Par. 1)
2. part ___section___ (Par 2)
3. counting each piece as a part of the total ___including___ (Par. 3)
4. rest ___relax___ (Par. 7)

In each row, circle the three words that belong together.

5. (cast) (crew) topics (producer)
6. (travel) parents (sports) (science)
7. city (camera) (film) (photography)
8. (speak) (discuss) (talk) turn

A word that means the opposite of another word is an **antonym.** Find an antonym in the story for each of the words below.

9. finish ___start___ (Par. 1)
10. scattered ___gathered___ (Par. 2)
11. calm ___nervous___ (Par. 6)
12. apart ___together___ (Par. 8)

Learning to Study

Circle the words in each column that would fit between the guide words.

1. **chew—cotton**
   (child)
   certain
   (comedy)
2. **refresh—rush**
   (regain)
   raise
   (rim)
3. **handle—huddle**
   hamper
   (hang)
   huge
4. **tape—transport**
   (tardy)
   (tax)
   trespass

Reading and Thinking

Write **C** before the groups of words that describe Carmen and **B** before the groups of words that describe Ben.

1. _C_ youngest of the cast members
2. _B_ worked on the show for three years
3. _B_ knows most of the cast members
4. _C_ has no experience on this show
5. _B_ works on a travel section
6. The groups of words below describe a character in the story. Write the character's name in the blank.
   oldest cast member   host of show
   ___Cindy___
7. Check the reason the author probably wrote this story.
   ___ to give facts about Ben's trip
   ✓ to give facts about the cast
   ___ to give facts about Carmen
8. How do you know that Carmen felt better after talking to the cast and crew?
   She thanked them for being so nice so
   she could stop being nervous.
   (Answers may vary.)

Working with Words

The prefix **mis-** means "badly." For example, *misbehave* means "to behave badly." Add **mis-** to each word. Then write the meaning of the new word.

1. _mis_ spell ___spell badly___
2. _mis_ match ___match badly___
3. _mis_ place ___place something badly; lose___
4. _mis_ read ___read badly___
5. _mis_ judge ___judge badly___

5

Knowing the Words

Write the words from the story that have the meanings below.

1. took a small drink ___sipped___ (Par. 7)
2. ideas or hints ___suggestions___ (Par. 9)
3. pretending ___faking___ (Par. 11)

Check the meaning of the underlined word in each sentence.

4. Mom was fixing the lamp when the telephone rang.
   ✓ repairing
   ___ preparing
5. My friend and I wanted to run for the same class office.
   ___ move quicker than walking
   ✓ be in an election
6. I left the stage after my speech.
   ___ opposite of "right"
   ✓ went away
7. Kate had a hard time making the chili.
   ___ solid
   ✓ difficult

Learning to Study

Write the number of the encyclopedia volume that would have the most information for each of these topics.

Vol. 1 A–C	Vol. 2 D–F	Vol. 3 G–J	Vol. 4 K–M	Vol. 5 N–Q	Vol. 6 R–T	Vol. 7 U–Z

1. _5_ presidents
2. _3_ horses
3. _1_ baseball
4. _2_ eagle
5. _7_ whales
6. _1_ bikes
7. _5_ nurses
8. _1_ cooking

Reading and Thinking

Write **T** before the sentences that are true. Write **F** before the sentences that are false.

1. _T_ Ben's mom is a nurse.
2. _F_ Kate had the idea to fix dinner.
3. _T_ Ben's mom asked about his meeting.
4. _F_ It was Ben's idea to go to the Baseball Hall of Fame.
5. _F_ The whole family will go to Washington, D.C.
6. _F_ Ling thought the trip should be planned at a later time.
7. Ben's dad could go with his children to Washington, D.C., because ___he___
   wouldn't start work until they returned
8. Why wasn't Ling surprised by Kate's idea about the Baseball Hall of Fame?
   She knew Kate liked baseball.
   (Answers may vary.)
9. How do you think Ben's mom feels about the family trip to Washington, D.C.?
   She is happy they can go.
   (Answers may vary.)

Working with Words

The prefix **non-** means "not." For example, *nonmetal* means "not metal." Add **non-** to each word below. Then write the meaning of the new word.

1. _non_ profit ___not making a profit___
2. _non_ stop ___not stopping___
3. _non_ electric ___not electric___

7

Knowing the Words

Write the words from the story that have the meanings below.

1. wonderful ___terrific___ (Par. 2)
2. forms of transportation ___vehicles___ (Par. 5)
3. first ___original___ (Par. 10)
4. emptied on the inside ___hollowed___ (Par. 14)
5. made ___constructed___ (Par. 14)

A word that means the opposite of another word is an **antonym.** Find an antonym in the story for each of the words below.

6. past ___future___ (Par. 3)
7. long ___brief___ (Par. 5)
8. removing ___bringing___ (Par. 7)
9. real ___fake___ (Par. 11)

Learning to Study

An **outline** is used to put ideas in order. It can be used to show important facts from a story. Use the facts from paragraph 12 to complete Part I. Then use the facts in paragraph 14 to complete Part II.

I. The White House is damaged and rebuilt   (Answers may vary.)
   A. Fire began by the British in 1814
   B. Rainstorm puts the fire out
   C. Inside is completely rebuilt
   D. Walls began to crack again
   E. White House could cave in

II. The White House is rebuilt again
   A. Walls are made stronger
   B. Inside built same as before
   C. Project took four years

Reading and Thinking

Circle the word that best completes each sentence.

1. The ___ is trained to give information to a tour group.
   worker (guide) tourist
2. Ben had to complete the ___ for his show before the deadline.
   path   company   (project)
3. Check the sentence that best states the main idea of the story.
   ___ The Wilkins family watches cars arrive at the White House.
   ✓ Ben sees and learns about the White House before the tour.
   ___ One President didn't live in the White House.

A **fact** is something that is known to be true. An **opinion** is what a person believes. It may or may not be true. Write **F** before the sentences that are facts. Write **O** before the sentences that are opinions.

4. _F_ People from many countries visit the White House.
5. _O_ Everyone would like to live in the White House.
6. _F_ The first White House was burned in 1814.
7. _O_ The British should have rebuilt the White House after it burned.

Working with Words

Think of the meaning of the prefix in each word. Then write the meaning of the word.

1. misshape ___shape badly___
2. presale ___sell before___
3. nonliving ___not living___

9

Knowing the Words

Write the words from the story that have the meanings below.

1. a place for burying _____ **tomb**
(Par. 4)
2. walking back and forth _____ **pacing**
(Par. 6)
3. looked at closely _____ **inspected**
(Par. 7)
4. a special service _____ **ceremony**
(Par. 7)
5. a test _____ **exam**
(Par. 9)

Abbreviations are shortened forms of words. Match the word in the first column with its abbreviation.

6. _c_ United States **a.** Mr.
7. _a_ Mister **b.** D.C.
8. _b_ District of Columbia **c.** U.S.

A **synonym** is a word with the same or nearly the same meaning as another word. Circle each pair of synonyms.

9. (guarded—protected) 12. (hurry—rush)
10. (tugged—pulled) 13. sit—stood
11. whispered—shouted 14. (piece—part)

Learning to Study

Use the facts from paragraph 7 to complete Part I. Then use paragraph 11 to complete Part II. (Answers may vary.)

I. Changing of the Guard
   A. Officer inspects rifle and uniform
   B. New guard begins pacing
   C. Officer and first guard leave

II. Guard Training
   A. Do precise marching
   B. Know cemetery history
   C. Give location of 200 burial plots

Reading and Thinking

1. What did Ling, Ben, Mr. Wilkins, and Kate see at Arlington National Cemetery?
   Changing of the Guard or first female guard

2. When is the Tomb of the Unknowns guarded?
   day and night

3. Why is the Tomb of the Unknowns guarded?
   to honor all the unknown soldiers
   who died in battle

4. Why is Sergeant Johnsen a history maker?
   She is the first female honor guard.

5. How do you think Ben felt about the job of becoming an honor guard?
   He thought it was difficult.

Working with Words

The prefixes **im-** and **in-** mean "not." For example, *impatient* means "not patient." *Inactive* means "not active." The prefix **im-** is usually used before words that begin with *b*, *m*, or *p*. The prefix **in-** is usually used before words that begin with other letters. Add **im-** or **in-** to each word below. Use each new word in a sentence.

1. _im_ possible _____
   (Sentences will vary.)

2. _in_ experience _____
   (Sentences will vary.)

3. _im_ balance _____
   (Sentences will vary.)

11

Knowing the Words

Write the words from the story that have the meanings below.

1. the overhead part of a room _____ **ceiling**
(Par. 4)
2. a type of rock _____ **limestone**
(Par. 4)
3. a force or weight _____ **pressure**
(Par. 8)

In each row, circle the words that belong together.

4. (listening) (noticing) (looking) ceiling
5. club (ore) (rocks) (limestone)
6. (helper) (assistant) (guide) level

7. A **simile** is a figure of speech. It compares two things using *like* or *as*. For example, *the sunshine felt like fire* is a simile. Write the simile used in paragraph 4.
   dripstones look like spears

Learning to Study

1. Complete the outline below. Use the facts from paragraph 3 to complete Part I. Use the facts from paragraph 4 to complete Part II. (Answers may vary.)

I. Early days of Mammoth Cave
   A. Visitors came on horseback and by stagecoach
   B. Ore prepared in caves

II. How dripstones are formed
   A. Water carries limestone
   B. Limestone builds into dripstones

Number the words in each column in alphabetical order.

2. _2_ lantern   3. _3_ million
   _3_ locate   _2_ midnight
   _1_ lane   _1_ mention

Reading and Thinking

1. Number the events to show the order in which they happened.
   _5_ Pam described blindfish.
   _2_ The guide told the tour group that folks came to Mammoth Cave by stagecoach.
   _1_ Mr. Wilkins suggested a trip to Mammoth Cave.
   _4_ The tour group learned about the Echo River.
   _3_ Pam gave a warning.

2. You shouldn't touch dripstones because
   they will stop growing

3. The fish in Mammoth Cave are called blindfish because they have no eyes

Write **E** before the sentences that tell about the early days of Mammoth Cave. Write **N** before the sentences that tell about Mammoth Cave now.

4. _N_ The cave is open for tours.
5. _E_ Ore used in gunpowder is prepared.
6. _N_ A tour includes a look at dripstones.
7. _E_ People ride horses to the cave.

Working with Words

Add **'s** to singular nouns to show a person or thing owns something. Make the noun after each sentence possessive. Then write that form in the sentence.

1. The _____ family's _____ tour through the cave was interesting. (family)

2. Pam knew the _____ club's _____ rules. (club)

3. The _____ guide's _____ stories made the tour interesting. (guide)

13

Knowing the Words

Write the words from the story that have the meanings below.

1. opening _____ **passage**
(Par. 5)
2. have great fear _____ **panic**
(Par. 5)
3. necessary supplies _____ **equipment**
(Par. 7)

A word that means the opposite of another word is an **antonym**. Write the pair of antonyms from each sentence.

4. The lantern's bright beam helped us to see through the dark passage of the cave.
   bright, dark

5. My friends often explore caves, but they seldom go without some club members.
   often, seldom

Learning to Study

A **table of contents** is on one of the first pages in a book. It shows the chapters that are in the book. It also shows the page each chapter begins on. Use the table of contents below to answer the questions.

Adventures Underground
Table of Contents

1. How many chapters are in the book?
   4

2. Write the title of the chapter that may tell about finding Mammoth Cave.
   Cave Discoveries

3. On what page does "Cave Beauty" begin?
   page 45

Reading and Thinking

Circle the word that best completes each sentence.

1. Because she liked caves, it was ___ for Pam to be the guide's assistant.
   popular (natural) necessary

2. The guide was ___ the cave tour.
   talking   pointing   (leading)

3. Check the sentence that best states the main idea of the story.
   _✓_ Pam discusses caving.
   ___ Cavers should tie their shoes.
   ___ Caving alone is dangerous.

4. Will Pam stay a caving club member?
   Why or why not? Yes, because she
   enjoys caving. (Answers may vary.)

5. What makes Pam good at guiding people through caves?
   She knows about caves and cave safety.

Working with Words

Add an apostrophe to the end of a plural noun that ends in **s** to show that a person or thing owns something. For example, the bones of the dogs would be written as *the dogs' bones*. Make the plural noun after each sentence possessive. Then use the possessive form of the word in the sentence.

1. We can still enjoy the _Native Americans'_ discoveries. (Native Americans)

2. The _explorers'_ equipment fills a van. (explorers)

3. Some _bats'_ habits are odd. (bats)

4. The _members'_ supplies were checked. (members)

15

Knowing the Words

Write the words from the story that have the meanings below.

1. pushing with your feet _____ **pedaling**
(Par. 1)
2. opening to something _____ **entrance**
(Par. 3)
3. picture from a camera _____ **photograph**
(Par. 4)

Check the meaning of the underlined word in each sentence.

4. The items for the sale were on a <u>stand</u> at the end of the counter.
   ___ be on your feet
   _✓_ table

5. Ann wore a costume to the party given by our <u>club</u>.
   ___ a large stick
   _✓_ a special group

Learning to Study

A newspaper **index** lists many sections that have information you may need or want. Write the number for the sections you would use to find the information listed below.

INDEX

Advertisements	G6–14
Business	E1–19
Entertainment	D1–12
City	B1–7
Sports	B8–17

1. last night's game score _____ B8–17

2. movie times _____ D1–12

3. mayor's meetings _____ B1–7

4. paper route job _____ G6–14

5. name of new factory manager _____ E1–19

6. closed city streets _____ B1–7

Reading and Thinking

Write **T** before the sentences that are true. Write **F** before the sentences that are false.

1. _T_ Ling likes to ride her bike.
2. _F_ Ling belongs to the Pedalers.
3. _F_ Ling heard from a friend that the bike club was in town.

4. What must bikers do to ride long trips?
   work hard to build their strength

5. Check the reason the author probably wrote this story.
   _✓_ to tell about a special club
   ___ to tell about Ling's flat tire
   ___ to tell about bike trails

6. A **summary** is a short sentence that tells about a topic. To make a summary you must find the most important facts. The sentence below is a summary for paragraph 6.
   The Glenns formed a bicycle club.

Underline the sentence below that is the best summary for paragraph 7.
   Bikers work hard to build strength.
   <u>The bike club takes long and short trips.</u>

Working with Words

A **compound word** is a word made by combining two smaller words. Write the two words that make up the underlined compound word in each sentence.

1. I asked two friends to stay <u>overnight</u> after we worked at the school play.
   over, night

2. Our class wrote a school <u>newspaper</u>.
   news, paper

17

Knowing the Words

Write the words from the story that have the meanings below.

1. talk between two or more people _____ conversation _____
   (Par. 3)

2. leaned _____ propped _____
   (Par. 5)

A word that sounds the same as another word but has a different spelling and meaning is a **homophone**. Draw a line under the homophone that correctly completes each sentence.

3. The ____ was still on the grass when Ling left to ride her bike. (dew, do)

4. The ____ a bike looks has changed over the years. (way, weigh)

5. Write the sentence from paragraph 7 that has a simile. _____ It looked like a wooden horse on wooden wheels. _____

Learning to Study

A **bar graph** is used to compare different things. This bar graph shows total distances traveled every year by the club. Answer the questions using the graph.

	Miles
Year 1	
Year 2	
Year 3	

Miles 0   500 1,000 1,500 2,000 2,500 3,000 3,500

1. In what year did the club travel over three thousand miles? _____ Year 3 _____

2. In what year did the club travel the least? _____ Year 2 _____

Reading and Thinking

1. Check the sentence that best states the main idea of the story.
   ___ Riding a bicycle is fun.
   ✓ Bikes have changed over the years.
   ___ Ling introduces a new friend.

2. Will bikes change in the future? Why or why not? _____ (Answers will vary.) _____

Write **M** before the words that could describe modern bicycles. Write **E** before words that could describe some of the early bicycles.

3. _E_ is pushed with the feet
4. _E_ has seat five feet off the ground
5. _M_ uses brakes
6. _E_ has wooden wheels

Write **F** before the sentences that are facts. Write **O** before the sentences that are opinions.

7. _O_ Bike riding is the best exercise.
8. _O_ Everyone enjoys riding a bike.
9. _F_ The first bike was invented over one hundred years ago.
10. _O_ All bikes should look the same.

Working with Words

Use two words from each sentence to make a compound word. Write the compound word in the blank.

1. The rain was so heavy during the storm, some streets were flooded.
   _____ rainstorm _____

2. The cables that are under the ground need to be fixed.
   _____ underground _____

19

Knowing the Words

Write the words from the story that have the meanings below.

1. a raised flat stand _____ platform _____
   (Par. 1)

2. small amount of running liquid _____ trickle _____
   (Par. 7)

3. kind of power _____ electricity _____
   (Par. 10)

A **synonym** is a word with the same or nearly the same meaning as another word. Write the pair of synonyms from each sentence.

4. The force of the falling water was used to make the power for the city.
   _____ force, power _____

5. He yelled directions to the girl as she shouted over the loud noise.
   _____ yelled, shouted _____

Learning to Study

Read the chart. Write **T** before the sentences that are true. Write **F** before the sentences that are false.

Niagara Falls Tourist Information			
	Number of Tourists		
States	1992	1994	1996
Maine	18,751	16,402	19,576
Ohio	35,783	37,914	43,587
Georgia	27,982	25,431	28,587

1. _F_ In 1992 most tourists came from Georgia.
2. _T_ More people from Maine came to the Falls in 1996 than in 1992.
3. _T_ Each year the fewest number of tourists came from Maine.
4. _F_ The number of tourists from Georgia was larger each year.

Reading and Thinking

1. Number the sentences to show the order in which things happened.
   _2_ Ben met Ling and the studio crew.
   _1_ Ben arrived at Niagara Falls.
   _5_ The crew stopped taping.
   _3_ The cast and crew toured the Cave of the Winds.
   _4_ Sections of the show were taped.

Circle the word that correctly completes each sentence.

2. A friend's opinion about an idea can ____ the way we think about that idea.
   meet (shape) believe

3. Cindy was ____ that Ling knew to meet her at the gate.
   confused upset (certain)

4. Where does this story take place?
   _____ Niagara Falls _____

5. What kind of power is made by using the water from the Falls?
   _____ electricity _____

6. Will Cindy and Robert need to give their reports on Niagara Falls again? Why or why not? _____
   _____ (Answers will vary.) _____

Working with Words

Underline the prefix in each word. Then write the meaning of the word.
(Answers may vary.)

1. inaction _____ no action _____
2. preview _____ look before _____
3. misjudge _____ judge badly _____

21

Knowing the Words

Write the words from the story that have the meanings below.

1. made changes _____ adjusted _____
   (Par. 4)
2. saved _____ rescued _____
   (Par. 9)
3. so loud you cannot hear _____ deafening _____
   (Par. 10)
4. very large _____ tremendous _____
   (Par. 11)

In each row, circle the words that belong together.

5. (rescued) wet (saved) (preserved)
6. (mist) (spray) rock (water)
7. believe (drive) (steer) (handle)
8. (problem) (trouble) chance (difficulty)
9. (stared) listened (looked) (noticed)

Learning to Study

1. Under what main topic in an encyclopedia could you find facts about both of these things?
   Maid of the Mist   Horseshoe Falls
   _____ Niagara Falls _____

2. What letter would you look under to find the volume with the best facts about the main topic you chose? _____ N _____
   (Answers may vary.)

The first word in dark print in each dictionary entry is the entry word. An entry word can have more than one meaning. Read the dictionary entry below. Then write the number of the meaning used in each of the sentences that follows.

roar /rōr/ n 1 the deep cry of a wild animal 2 a loud continuing sound

3. _2_ We heard the roar of the water before we could see the Falls.
4. _1_ The lion's roar surprised us.

Reading and Thinking

1. Check the sentence that best states the main idea of the story.
   ✓ The cast learns about a rescue.
   ___ Ben knows life jackets can save your life.
   ___ Being a captain on the *Maid of the Mist* takes training.

2. When did the *Maid of the Mist* begin sailing at the Falls? _____ 1846 _____

3. The boy went over the Falls because _he_ fell into the water after his boat sank

4. The rock under the Falls wears away because _____ the force of the water is strong _____.

5. Check the words that describe the captain.
   ✓ honest   ___ shy
   ___ friendly   ✓ trained

6. How was the boy's experience described by the captain different from the experience of others who went over the Falls? _____ He lived. Others died. _____
   (Answers may vary.)

Working with Words

A suffix is a group of letters added to the end of a base word to change its meaning. The suffix -ous can mean "has much." For example, *famous* means "has much fame." Add -ous to each word. Then write the meaning of the new word.

1. joy_ous_ _____ has much joy _____
2. humor_ous_ _____ has much humor _____

23

Knowing the Words

Write the words from the story that have the meanings below.

1. below something _____ underneath _____
   (Par. 5)
2. comes down _____ descends _____
   (Par. 6)
3. are present _____ attend _____
   (Par. 10)

Check the meaning of the underlined word in each sentence.

4. Since the owner knew how to <u>handle</u> a hot air balloon, Kim felt safe when she took her ride.
   ___ something used to control
   ✓ able to take care of something

5. The girls were <u>admitted</u> to the show after they bought their tickets.
   ___ say you know or feel something
   ✓ allowed to enter

6. Kim asked her aunt if she could <u>watch</u> the race from the air.
   ___ something that keeps time
   ✓ see

Learning to Study

An encyclopedia contains facts about many topics. Facts about the same main topic may be listed under different words. Kim wants to know more about other kinds of air transportation. Write three topics that she could use to find the facts she wants. Do not write *hot air balloons* as one of your topics.

1. _____
2. _____ (Answers will vary.) _____
3. _____

Reading and Thinking

Write **F** before the sentences that are facts. Write **O** before the sentences that are opinions.

1. _F_ People race hot air balloons.
2. _O_ No one likes to ride in a hot air balloon.
3. _F_ Hot air balloons can't be steered.
4. _F_ More people attend the festival now than when it started.
5. _O_ If you own a hot air balloon, you would like the balloon fiesta.

6. Check the reason the author probably wrote this story.
   ___ to give the history of the hot air balloon
   ✓ to tell about hot air ballooning
   ___ to tell about New Mexico

7. What happens when the heater under the basket warms the air inside the balloon? _____ The balloon goes up. _____

8. Write a sentence the author used to make you think Ben and Kim might fly in a hot air balloon. _____ Kim and I are floating high in the New Mexico sky. _____
   (Answers may vary.)

Working with Words

The suffix **-ment** can mean "the act of." For example, *announcement* means "the act of announcing." Add **-ment** to the base words. Then write the meaning of the new word.

1. enjoy _____ ment _____ the act of enjoying _____
2. agree _____ ment _____ the act of agreeing _____
3. measure _____ ment _____ the act of measuring _____
4. arrange _____ ment _____ the act of arranging _____

25

Write the words from the story that have the meanings below.

1. boat that carries people or cargo across water __ferry__
(Par. 4)

2. hat with a rounded shape __derby__
(Par. 8)

3. figure with three sides __triangle__
(Par. 10)

A word that means the opposite of another word is an **antonym.** Find an antonym in the story for each of the words below.

4. shouted __whispered__
(Par. 1)

5. brave __afraid__
(Par. 4)

6. downward __upward__
(Par. 10)

7. ordinary __unusual__
(Par. 12)

8. frowned __grinned__
(Par. 14)

Learning to Study

Read the directions below and answer the questions.

Drive through town going south and turn left at the first stoplight. Go straight for seven blocks and turn right at the service station on the corner. If you pass the library, you missed the turn. I live in the second to the last house on the right.

1. In what direction do you need to go to get to the first stoplight?
__south__

2. What would you pass if you've missed the turn? __library__

3. Is the house on the right or left side of the street? __right__

Reading and Thinking

Circle the word that correctly completes each sentence.

1. Every week the restaurant has a ___ dinner prepared for a lower price.
plate (special) burnt

2. I gave the rusty door a strong ___.
yell stare (tug)

3. Check the sentence that best states the main idea of the story.
___ Nantucket is a famous island.
_✓_ Nantucket has a lot to discover.
___ Nantucket has a whaling museum.

4. Where can Ben get his whaling questions answered?
__at the whaling museum__

5. What was the Kiteman's real name?
__Al Hartig__

6. Why are all of the Kiteman's kites different? __They are made by hand.__

7. What do you think Ben will discover in Nantucket? __(Answers will vary.)__

Working with Words

The suffix **-less** can mean "to be without." For example, *worthless* means "to be without worth." Add **-less** to each base word below. Use each new word in a sentence.

1. smoke __less__ _____
(Sentences will vary.)

2. care __less__ _____
(Sentences will vary.)

Knowing the Words

Write the words from the story that have the meanings below.

1. covering of a fish __scales__
(Par. 3)

2. bumps __knobs__
(Par. 4)

3. to be grateful __appreciate__
(Par. 4)

4. very large __immense__
(Par. 7)

A word that is spelled the same as another word but has a completely different meaning is a **homograph.** For each pair of meanings below, write one of the homographs that is listed.

point   scales   kind

5. a. nice
b. a type of something
__kind__

6. a. to show using a finger
b. the tip
__point__

7. a. instruments used for weighing
b. covering of a fish
__scales__

Learning to Study

Complete the following outline. Use paragraph 3 to complete Part I. Use paragraph 4 to complete Part II.
(Answers may vary.)

I. Humpback whales are like people
A. __Breathe through lungs__
B. __Have skin instead of scales__

II. Humpbacks needed protection
A. __Killed by hunters__
B. __Protected by 1966 law__

Reading and Thinking

Write **T** before the sentences that are true.
Write **F** before the sentences that are false.

1. _T_ Whales use their lungs to breathe.
2. _T_ Whales needed protection.
3. _F_ Whales are large fish.
4. _F_ Humpback whales have smooth heads.

5. Why did Ben change his opinion about studying whales? __He learned that__
__whales are interesting.__
(Answers may vary.)

6. Why are there more humpback whales today than there were before 1966?
__The law protects the whales from__
__hunters so more whales live longer.__
(Answers may vary.)

Write **B** before the facts Ben knew about the whales before he talked to the captain.
Write **A** before the facts Ben knew after he talked to the captain.

7. _A_ The heads of humpbacks have knobs.
8. _B_ Whales aren't fish.
9. _B_ Whales have skin.
10. _A_ A law was passed in 1966 to protect humpback whales.

Working with Words

The suffix **-able** means "capable of." For example, *affordable* is "capable of being afforded." Add **-able** to each word below. Use each new word in a sentence.

1. punish __able__ _____
(Sentences will vary.)

2. defend __able__ _____
(Sentences will vary.)

Knowing the Words

Write the words from the story that have the meanings below.

1. personal book of writing __journal__
(Par. 1)

2. well-known places __landmarks__
(Par. 6)

3. people who live in the colonies __colonists__
(Par. 6)

4. chance __opportunity__
(Par. 8)

A **synonym** is a word with the same or nearly the same meaning as another word. Write the words from the story that are synonyms for these words.

5. drop __dump__
(Par. 6)

6. goods __cargo__
(Par. 6)

7. evening __night__
(Par. 8)

Learning to Study

Reading maps makes it easier to find your way. Read a map Ben could use as he walks the Freedom Trail. Then answer the questions.

1. If Ben walks west from the statue of Benjamin Franklin, what is the next building he'll see? __State House__

2. In what direction should you walk to go from the State House to the Old West Church? __north__

Reading and Thinking

1. Number the events to show the order in which they happened.
_3_ Ben wrote in his journal.
_1_ Ben walked the Freedom Trail.
_5_ Ben traveled back to Chicago.
_2_ Ben said he was tired.
_4_ Ben fell asleep after a long day.

2. Check the sentence that best states the main idea of the story.
___ Ben doesn't like to walk.
___ Paul Revere is important in history.
_✓_ Ben learns about Boston's history.

3. The lanterns were hung in the Old North Church because __the colonists__
__needed to know when the British__
__were attacking__

4. A summary includes important facts about a topic. The sentence below is a summary for paragraph 6.
Boston has many historical landmarks.
Underline the sentence below that is the best summary for paragraph 7.
Paul Revere's ride is in the history books.
__Lanterns at a church warned the colonists of an attack.__

Working with Words

Underline the suffix in each word. Then write the meaning of the word.

1. pay<u>able</u> __able to be paid__
2. mountain<u>ous</u> __full of mountains__
3. price<u>less</u> __without a price__
4. accept<u>able</u> __can be accepted__

Knowing the Words

Write the words from the story that have the meanings below.

1. strong __sturdy__
(Par. 6)

2. something that sends back light __reflectors__
(Par. 9)

3. not modern __old-fashioned__
(Par. 13)

Check the meaning of the underlined homograph as it is used in the sentence.

4. The sales clerk returned my <u>change</u>.
_✓_ money from a larger amount
___ make different from what is

5. I learned to <u>cast</u> the fishing line by watching my friend.
___ people who act in a show
_✓_ throw

Learning to Study

Use the table of contents below to answer the questions

Early Lighthouses

1. What is the title of the first chapter?
__Boston Light__

2. What chapter would tell how lighthouses look? __Lighthouse Designs__

3. What pages could you read to find out about the lighthouse Ben saw? __1–24__

4. On what pages would you find facts about safety problems in lighthouses?
__65–78__

Reading and Thinking

Write **T** before the sentences that are true.
Write **F** before the sentences that are false.

1. _T_ Boston Light was built in 1716.
2. _F_ No lighthouses have been destroyed by fire.
3. _T_ Coal fires were used in lighthouses.
4. _F_ Lighthouses always saved ships.
5. _T_ Some lighthouses use computers.

6. Do you think many lighthouses have been destroyed by fire in the last fifty years? Why or why not? _____
__(Answers will vary.)__

7. Even with modern lighthouses, ships may still wreck because __they have trouble__
__on rough and stormy seas__

8. Check the reason the author probably wrote this story.
___ to tell about sea rescues
_✓_ to give facts about lighthouses
___ to give facts about Maine

Working with Words

Fill in each blank with the possessive form of the word in parentheses.

1. We learned the __seaport's__ history. (seaport)

2. The __lighthouse's__ purpose was to warn ships of dangers. (lighthouse)

3. The __ship's__ wreck may not have happened if the captain had followed the lighthouse beam. (ship)

4. The __computer's__ program keeps the lighthouse working. (computer)

Knowing the Words

Write the words from the story that have the meanings below.

1. confused heap ___mess___
   (Par. 9)
2. to have clipped wool ___sheared___
   (Par. 10)

In each row, circle the words that belong together.

3. (college) (school) (university) report
4. (kitchen) village (hall) (lobby)
5. (searching) (seeking) (looking) sleeping

6. An **idiom** is a group of words that has a special meaning. For example, *to give someone a hand* means "to help someone." Write the idiom found in paragraph 7 that has the meaning below.

go away ___take a hike___

Learning to Study

Number the words in each column in alphabetical order.

1. _1_ machine   2. _3_ velvet
   _3_ melt   _2_ vase
   _2_ match   _1_ valley

Read a map of a historical village to answer the questions.

3. What building do you go through to enter the village? ___General Store___
4. What two shops are closest to the exit?
   ___print shop and candle shop___

Reading and Thinking

Circle the word that best completes each sentence.

1. The man ___ about the broken lamp.
   regained (complained) realized
2. Ben had to keep his ___ when he stood on the beam.
   (balance) report exit
3. Check the words that describe Kate.
   ✓ helpful   ___ selfish
   ___ shy   ✓ funny

Write **F** before the sentences that are facts. Write **O** before the sentences that are opinions.

4. _F_ Sturbridge Village is a historical village.
5. _O_ It would be fun to live in a historical village.
6. _O_ It was harder to do things in the 1700s than it is to do things now.
7. _F_ Sturbridge Village is in New England.
8. Do you think Ben will change his room so he can more easily find what he needs? Why or why not? _____
   (Answers will vary.)

Working with Words

Fill in the blank with the possessive form of the word in parentheses.

1. Ben read about the ___visitors'___ experiences. (visitors)
2. The ___stores'___ owners were dressed in costumes. (stores)
3. The ___brothers'___ ideas were used to make the village. (brothers)

35

Knowing the Words

Write the words from the story that have the meanings below.

1. spread out awkwardly ___sprawled___
   (Par. 5)
2. tried ___attempted___
   (Par. 5)
3. twist into a mess ___tangle___
   (Par. 5)
4. moved smoothly ___glided___
   (Par. 11)

A word that means the opposite of another word is an **antonym.** Write the pair of antonyms from each sentence.

5. Kate steadied her skis, but then they wobbled and she began to fall.
   ___steadied, wobbled___
6. Kate slipped backward on the slope when she tried to move forward.
   ___backward, forward___
7. What do you think the words *couldn't believe his eyes* mean in paragraph 12?
   ___couldn't believe what he was seeing___
   (Answers may vary.)

Working with Words

Form a compound word by writing one of the words from the list in each blank.

line base flake

1. snow ___flake___
2. ___base___ ball
3. side ___line___

Use each compound word from above in a sentence.

4. _____
5. ___(Sentences will vary.)___
6. _____

Reading and Thinking

Write **K** before phrases about Kate. Write **B** before phrases about Ben.

1. _K_ enjoys skiing
2. _B_ thinks skiing might be hard
3. _K_ learns to get up after falling
4. _K_ skis down beginners' slope
5. _B_ falls over crossed skis
6. Write a sentence from the story that tells you Kate skied before Ben.
   ___"Wait until you try it, Ben," shouted___
   ___Kate as she glided past her brother.___
7. Underline the sentence below that is the best summary for paragraph 5.
   Ben was surprised to see Kate fall.
   Kate fell and couldn't get up.

Learning to Study

Use the information on the poster to answer the questions.

All-Day Rentals	
Boots	$ 9.10
Skis	$13.00
Poles	$ 5.00
All equipment	$15.00
(Boots, Skis, Pole)	

1. Can Ben rent all the equipment he needs for skiing? ___yes___
2. How much would it cost to rent skis?
   ___$13.00___
3. How long can you use the equipment you rent? ___all day___
4. What equipment has the lowest rental cost? ___poles___

37

Knowing the Words

Write the words from the story that have the meanings below.

1. giving hope ___encouragement___
   (Par. 3)
2. helpful suggestion ___advice___
   (Par. 5)

Draw a line to match each homophone with its meaning.

3. close   food from an animal
4. clothes   the opposite of *yes*
5. know   to shut
6. no   things worn on the body
7. meet   to have certain information
8. meat   to join

Learning to Study

Entry words are divided into syllables to show where the words can be divided at the end of a line of writing. Write these words in syllables.

1. bottom ___bot / tom___
2. tangle ___tan / gle___
3. mountain ___moun / tain___

The graph shows how much snow fell three days before Ben went skiing. Read the graph. Then answer the questions.

Snowfall
Wednesday: ▉
Thursday: ▉▉
Friday: ▉
Inches: 0 2 4 6 8

4. What day had the most snowfall?
   ___Thursday___
5. What is the largest snowfall, in inches, recorded on the graph? ___6 inches___

Reading and Thinking

1. Check the sentence that best states the main idea of the story.
   ___ Cindy introduces a friend.
   ✓ Determined people can succeed.
   ___ Skiing takes balance and practice.
2. Cindy introduces Pat to Ben because
   ___she thinks Pat can encourage Ben___
   (Answers may vary.)
3. Pat practices so hard because ___she___ ___wants to try out for the U.S. Disabled___ ___Ski Team___.
4. What do you think Ben will do after watching and talking to Cindy's friend?
   _____
   (Answers will vary.)
5. Circle the words that describe Pat.
   (strong) lazy (helpful) (friendly)

Working with Words

Check the correct meaning of the underlined word.

1. Cindy knew Ben needed <u>encouragement</u> when she found him in the snow.
   ✓ act of encouraging
   ___ not encouraging
   ___ full of courage
2. The ski slopes are in a <u>mountainous</u> area.
   ✓ not a mountain
   ___ full of mountains
   ___ small mountains
3. He thought learning to ski was <u>hopeless</u>.
   ✓ without hope
   ___ having hope
   ___ giving hope

39

Knowing the Words

Write the words from the story that have the meanings below.

1. study ___explore___
   (Par. 9)
2. items for sale ___goods___
   (Par. 11)
3. information storage ___memory___
   (Par. 13)

Check the meaning of the underlined word in each sentence.

4. The park was so crowded there was no <u>room</u> to move.
   ___ part of a house
   ✓ space able to be used
5. The ladder had a weak <u>step</u> and was not safe to use.
   ✓ rung or stair
   ___ lifting the foot and placing it down in a new place

Learning to Study

A library's card catalog or computer reference system can be used to help you find a book. Books are usually organized three ways in a card catalog or computer reference system. One way is by subject or main topic. Ben wants to know more about robots. Write two subjects he can look up to find books about robots. Do not write *robots* as one of your topics.

1. ___Answers will vary but may include machines___
2. ___Answers will vary but may include computers___

Reading and Thinking

1. Number the events to show the order in which they happened.
   _2_ Ben and Kate ate breakfast.
   _4_ Kate said she needs a robot.
   _3_ Kate began to clean her room.
   _1_ Ben awakened his sister.
   _5_ Kate told how robots help people.

Write **T** before the sentences that are true. Write **F** before the sentences that are false.

2. _F_ Robots think like people.
3. _T_ Ben and Kate started to clean their rooms.
4. _T_ Voices control some robots.
5. _F_ Ben explained how robots work.
6. _T_ Kate saw a movie about robots.
7. Do you think Ben likes to tease Kate? Why or why not? _____
   (Answers will vary.)
8. Do you think Kate will ever own a robot? Why or why not? _____
   (Answers will vary.)

Working with Words

Check the correct meaning of the underlined word.

1. The <u>imperfect</u> machine should be fixed.
   ___ perfect before
   ✓ not perfect
   ___ always perfect
2. My sister attends a <u>preschool</u> each day.
   ✓ before school
   ___ near school
   ___ after school

41

Knowing the Words

Write the words from the story that have the meanings below.

1. marked by the post office __postmarked__
   (Par. 1)

2. anxiously __eagerly__
   (Par. 1)

3. made bigger than it really is __exaggerated__
   (Par. 5)

4. something bought or given as a reminder __souvenir__
   (Par. 8)

A **synonym** is a word with the same or nearly the same meaning as another word. Circle each pair of synonyms.

5. (large—huge)   10. awkward—respect
6. noisy—quiet   11. (admire—respect)
7. talk—hear   12. (action—motion)
8. slam—open   13. (picture—drawing)
9. (ask—inquire)   14. friend—enemy

15. Choose one of the synonym pairs above. Use the two synonyms in a sentence. _____
   (Sentences will vary.)

Learning to Study

Complete the following outline. Use the facts in paragraph 5 to complete Part I. Use the facts in paragraph 6 to complete Part II.
(Answers may vary.)

I. Pictures for a cartoon
   A. Twenty-four per second
   B. 1,440 per minute
   C. Fewer pictures make motion awkward

II. Cartoon actions
   A. Lip motions drawn to match words
   B. Pictures match noisy actions

Reading and Thinking

Circle the word that best completes each sentence.

1. The plow was ____ by a team of horses.
   carried   (drawn)   pushed

2. The cartoonist drew the ____ of the title.
   (letters)   souvenirs   sounds

3. Check the sentence that best states the main idea of the story.
   ____ Ben likes to write letters.
   ____ Paul likes to draw cartoons.
   ✓ Cartoonists are talented workers.

4. Do you think Ben will encourage Paul to keep drawing cartoons? Why or why not?
   _____
   _____
   (Answers will vary.)

Write **T** before the sentences that are true. Write **F** before the sentences that are false.

5. _F_ Pete draws cartoons for movies.
6. _F_ Ben wrote to Paul from home.
7. _T_ Cartoon pictures match lip motions.
8. _T_ Each cartoon tells a story.

Working with Words

Check the correct meaning of the underlined word.

1. The girl gave an incorrect answer.
   ____ always correct
   ____ corrected after
   ✓ not correct

2. Paula is in the entertainment business.
   ____ one who entertains
   ✓ act of entertaining
   ____ entertain before

43

Knowing the Words

Write the words from the story that have the meanings below.

1. someone who offers to help __volunteer__
   (Par. 1)

2. furry animal that looks like a small bear __koala__
   (Par. 6)

3. knowing __aware__
   (Par. 9)

4. A simile compares two things using *like* or *as*. Write the simile in paragraph 7.
   It certainly looks like a teddy bear.

For each pair of meanings below, write one of the homographs that is listed.

   count   spotted   check

5. a. something used as money
   b. to make sure
   __check__

6. a. say numbers in order
   b. a person in a high position
   __count__

7. a. located
   b. marked with stains
   __spotted__

Working with Words

Read words 1–4 and underline the prefix in each word. Then complete each sentence with one of the words.

1. predate   3. incapable
2. mistrust   4. impersonal

5. I would __mistrust__ someone who lied.
6. Because I am not trained, I am __incapable__ of doing the job.

Reading and Thinking

Complete each sentence with the correct word or words from the story.

1. In what city is the zoo located?
   San Diego

2. What did Kate see in a tree?
   a koala

3. Where do koalas come from?
   Australia

4. What kind of animals do zoo volunteers handle? __tame animals__

5. What do you think Ben learned from working with animals for his show?
   (Answers will vary.)

6. Do you think Ben will work with animals for his show again? Why or why not?
   _____
   (Answers will vary.)

Learning to Study

Complete the following outline. Use the facts from paragraph 7 to complete Part I. Use the facts from paragraph 9 to complete Part II.
(Answers may vary.)

I. The koala
   A. Looks like a teddy bear
   B. Comes from Australia
   C. Eats certain kinds of leaves

II. Taping Ben's show
   A. Beth began explanation
   B. Rabbit jumped from Beth
   C. Rabbit was chased
   D. Rabbit was found unharmed

45

Knowing the Words

Write the words from the story that have the meanings below.

1. winner of a contest __champion__
   (Par. 7)

2. something used to shape things __mold__
   (Par. 9)

3. rounded __arched__
   (Par. 9)

4. something made with great skill __masterpiece__
   (Par. 11)

Write the words from the story that would use these abbreviations.

5. CA __California__
   (Par. 1)

6. BC __British Columbia__
   (Par. 7)

In each row, circle the words that belong together.

7. (shape)   (mold)   (build)   blanket
8. (sand)   hotel   (beach)   (water)

Learning to Study

An **index** lists a book's topics in alphabetical order. It also lists page numbers to help you find the topics. Use the index below to answer the questions.

Sand castles, 4, 9–12
Sand contests, 13–15
Sand shapes, 1–8

1. What pages would show different shapes that can be formed from sand?
   pages 1–8

2. On what pages can information about sand castles be found? __pages 4, 9–12__

3. Under what topic would you look to find facts about a sand building championship?
   sand contests

Reading and Thinking

1. Check the sentence that best states the main idea of the story.
   ✓ Sand can be used to build shapes for contests or for fun.
   ____ There is a certain way to work with sand.
   ____ The beach is the best place to do sand building.

2. Why do you keep the sand wet? __so it holds its shape__

Write **F** before the sentences that are facts. Write **O** before the sentences that are opinions.

3. _O_ Everyone can build a sand castle.
4. _F_ The weight of sand can be heavy.
5. _O_ Sand building contests are fun.
6. _F_ The tide can ruin a sand shape.

7. Underline the summary for paragraph 7.
   Ben and Kate meet a champion sand castle builder.
   Mr. Kirk won a world championship.

8. Underline the summary for paragraph 9.
   Grandpa Wilkins helps with the castle.
   Four workers build a sand castle.

Working with Words

Circle the prefix in each underlined word. Then write the underlined word and its meaning.

1. The (im)perfect towels were on sale.
   imperfect—not perfect

2. Mr. Kirk gave Ben a (non)fiction book about the history of sand castles.
   nonfiction—not fiction

47

Knowing the Words

Write the words from the story that have the meanings below.

1. thinking of new things __imagination__
   (Par. 2)

2. times to come __future__
   (Par. 4)

3. used arm movements __motioned__
   (Par. 7)

Check the meaning of the underlined word in each sentence.

4. I bought a watch at the jewelry store.
   ✓ something used to keep time
   ____ look

5. He had to board the tour bus twice.
   ✓ get on something
   ____ a piece of wood

Learning to Study

Many words have more than one part of speech. Some dictionaries give definitions of each part of speech in a separate entry. Symbols for two parts of speech are *n* = *noun* and *v* = *verb*. Use the dictionary entries below to answer the questions.

¹**building** /bil'ding/ *n* something built
²**building** /bil'ding/ *v* make or put together

1. What part of speech is the word in the first entry? __noun__

2. What does the word *building* mean when it is used as a verb?
   make or put together

3. Number the words in alphabetical order.
   _3_ scrap   _6_ seal
   _5_ scream   _4_ scratch
   _1_ sandy   _2_ scramble

Reading and Thinking

1. Number the events to show the order in which they happened.
   _3_ Mrs. Wilkins told about her visit.
   _5_ Ben's father teased Ben.
   _2_ Ben met the guide.
   _4_ Jeff talked about the new rides.
   _1_ Ben's family enjoyed a ride.

2. Check the sentence that best states the main idea of this story.
   ____ Ben likes Space Mountain.
   ✓ Tomorrowland is always changing.
   ____ Rocket Rods will be a fast ride.

Circle the word that best completes each sentence.

3. The first ____ of the film is exciting.
   (scene)   approach   cover

4. On Sundays, my brother ____ his boat to his favorite fishing spot.
   throws   (rows)   recognizes

5. Check the reason the author probably wrote this story.
   ____ to tell about Walt Disney
   ✓ to tell about Tomorrowland
   ____ to tell about fun rides

Working with Words

Use two words from each sentence to make a compound word. Write the compound word in the blank.

1. Kate must wear her glasses in the sun.
   sunglasses

2. The child felt the earth start to quake.
   earthquake

49

Knowing the Words

Write the words from the story that have the meanings below.

1. having a good result __successful__
   (Par. 2)
2. idea __theory__
   (Par. 2)
3. a type of airplane with no motor __glider__
   (Par. 2)

A word that means the opposite of another word is an **antonym.** Write the pair of antonyms from each sentence.

4. The wings of the plane were designed to be straight, but when they moved they looked crooked.
   __straight, crooked__
5. The Wrights repaired the plane after it was damaged during the flight.
   __repaired, damaged__

Learning to Study

Use this chart to answer the questions.

Wright Brothers' First Flight		
	Orville's Flight	Wilbur's Flight
Distance	120 feet	852 feet
Time	12 seconds	59 seconds
Date	December 17	December 17

1. Who flew the longest distance? __Wilbur__
2. How much time did the shorter flight take? __12 seconds__
3. What was the distance of Orville's flight? __120 feet__

Reading and Thinking

1. Check the sentence that best states the main idea of the story.
   ___ Robert wants to be a pilot.
   _✓_ Robert writes a report about famous pilots.
   ___ Robert wants to design planes.
2. Why didn't Wilbur Wright make the first flight? __A wing broke before the__ __plane could take off. After the repair,__ __it was Orville's turn to fly.__
3. Do you think airplanes will continue to be improved? Why or why not? _____
   (Answers will vary.)

Write **F** before the sentences that are facts. Write **O** before the sentences that are opinions.

4. _F_ The first successful airplane flight was in 1903.
5. _O_ The Wright brothers had the best plane.
6. _F_ A woman flew more than twenty-one miles across the English Channel.
7. _O_ The Wright brothers are the most important men in the history of flight.

Working with Words

Fill in each blank with the possessive form of the word in parentheses.

1. Some __women's__ ideas have helped to improve modern flight. (women)
2. The __men's__ airplane designs were judged. (men)

51

Knowing the Words

Write the words from the story that have the meanings below.

1. hole around the opening of a volcano __crater__
   (Par. 4)
2. blast __explosion__
   (Par. 8)

Check the meaning of the underlined homograph as it is used in the sentence.

3. Carmen wanted to __fly__ to Washington.
   ___ an insect
   _✓_ to travel by plane
4. The records had to be kept in the office __safe__ until the meeting.
   _✓_ special box for valuables
   ___ free from harm
5. Write the simile found in paragraph 8.
   __The force of the explosion was like a__ __bomb.__

Learning to Study

Use the entry below to answer the questions.

trunk/trungk/ n **1** the main part of a tree; **2** a box with a lid used when traveling

1. Write the first definition listed in the entry. __the main part of a tree__
2. Underline the sentence in which *trunk* has the same meaning as the second definition.
   __The trunk was packed for the trip.__
   The bark fell from the trunk of the tree.
3. Write a sentence that uses *trunk* meaning "the main part of a tree."
   (Sentences will vary.)

Reading and Thinking

1. Number the events to show the order in which they happened.
   _5_ Ash from the volcano was found hundreds of miles away.
   _1_ Plates of rock shifted under the mountain.
   _3_ The volcano exploded.
   _2_ Pressure built up as gas formed.
   _4_ Animals and trees were destroyed.

Circle the word that best completes each sentence.

2. The owner wanted to ____ the shop.
   trust   cut   (close)
3. I like to ____ in that chair.
   (rock)   knock   tracks
4. The railroad ____ were fixed.
   pilots   mountains   (tracks)
5. How does Cindy feel about flying over a volcano? __She feels scared when she__ __thinks of it. (Answers may vary.)__
6. Write the name of the character these words describe.
   trusting   excited   curious
   Carmen

Working with Words

Fill in each blank with the possessive form of the word in parentheses.

1. The __scientists'__ journals were discussed at the annual meeting in Boston. (scientists)
2. __Pilots'__ licenses are to be bought before Monday. (pilots)

53

Knowing the Words

Write the words from the story that have the meanings below.

1. promise __guarantee__
   (Par. 9)
2. tricks that are practiced __stunts__
   (Par. 9)
3. to throw and catch many things at one time __juggle__
   (Par. 9)

Check the meaning of the underlined word in each sentence.

4. Some schools __train__ students to act.
   _✓_ teach
   ___ a type of transportation
5. My friend took a __course__ at night school to learn acting.
   ___ direction or path
   _✓_ class taken to learn

Learning to Study

You can use a computer reference system or a card catalog to help you find a book you want. One way books are organized in a card catalog or computer reference system is by title. Use the information below to answer questions.

CALL NO: 791.335
AUTHOR: Stone, Mary
MAIN TITLE: Clowns and the Circus
PUBLISHER: Greenwillow, 1994

1. What is the title of the book? __Clowns__ __and the Circus__
2. What is the last name of the author? __Stone__

Reading and Thinking

1. Who wrote the letters Ling was reading?
   __the viewers__
2. What was one suggestion for Ben's show?
   __(Answers will vary.)__
3. What show ideas did Laurie like?
   __cooking school for kids and the__ __juggling contest__
4. Where is the Clown College?
   __Venice, Florida__
5. Check the sentence that best states the main idea of the story.
   ___ Viewers' ideas are discussed.
   ___ Juggling is a difficult skill.
   _✓_ You can learn how to be a clown.
6. Why was Laurie at the studio late? __Her__ __mom was late.__
7. Do you think Ling will use the idea about the clown college for the show? Why or why not? _____
   (Answers will vary.)

Working with Words

Fill in each blank with the possessive form of the word in parentheses.

1. The __viewers'__ letters expressed many good ideas for the TV show. (viewers)
2. Some of the __jugglers'__ acts were judged today. (jugglers)
3. The __clowns'__ costumes are chosen with care. (clowns)

55

Knowing the Words

Write the words from the story that have the meanings below.

1. lifted __scooped__
   (Par. 1)
2. a water activity __snorkeling__
   (Par. 5)
3. usual kind or type __typical__
   (Par. 5)
4. tube used to breathe underwater __snorkel__
   (Par. 5)

A word that means the opposite of another word is an **antonym.** Find an antonym in the story for each of the words below.

5. ordinary __special__
   (Par. 1)
6. leave __stay__
   (Par. 3)
7. sink __float__
   (Par. 6)

Learning to Study

Mrs. Wilkins used this schedule to help her choose her flight home to Chicago. Read the schedule and answer the questions.

Central Airlines Orlando to Chicago		
Flight	Leaves	Arrives
602	9:30 A.M.	10:30 A.M.
348	1:00 P.M.	2:00 P.M.
521	7:30 P.M.	8:30 P.M.

1. This schedule is for flights from Orlando to what city? __Chicago__
2. Which flight could she take if she wants to travel in the morning? __602__
3. If she takes Flight 348, when will she arrive? __2:00 P.M.__
4. Can she be home before 10:00 A.M.?
   __No__

Reading and Thinking

Circle the word that best completes each sentence.

1. The strong ____ carried the swimmer toward the shore.
   snorkel   (wave)   fish
2. We decorated the ____ for the parade.
   table   scoop   (float)
3. Why did Sue take lessons before she went snorkeling? __to learn to snorkel safely__
   (Answers may vary.)
4. Why should you blow water out of the snorkel? __so you don't get a mouthful__ __of water (Answers may vary.)__

Write **X** before the groups of words that describe Chicago. Write **Y** before the groups of words that describe Florida.

5. _Y_ where Mrs. Wilkins visited
6. _X_ home of the Wilkins family
7. _X_ is not on the ocean
8. _Y_ has coral off the coast
9. _Y_ good place for snorkeling

Working with Words

Write a compound word using two words from each sentence.

1. A boat that runs on steam is called a __steamboat__
2. A bell that you ring at a door is called a __doorbell__
3. Something used to mark a place in a book is called a __bookmark__

57

Knowing the Words

Write the words from the story that have the meanings below.

1. interest _____appeal_____
   (Par. 1)
2. area used for protection _____preserve_____
   (Par. 9)
3. units of land _____acres_____
   (Par. 9)

Write a word from the story that matches each of these abbreviations.

4. FL _____Florida_____
5. Mon. _____Monday_____

In each row, circle the words that belong together.

6. (rides) (shows) (games) meeting
7. camera (birds) (bugs) (alligators)
8. (friends) (family) tour (neighbors)

Learning to Study

Tess had some questions about wildlife after she'd spent the day at the nature preserve. She checked a book out from the library. Read part of her book's index and answer the questions.

> Alligators, 18–19
> Birds, 1–16, 33–67
> Insects, 68–102
> Nature preserves, 103–132

1. Under what topic could Tess look to find facts about bugs? _____insects_____
2. What topic is covered in two different places in the book? _____birds_____
3. On what pages might Tess find facts about the nature preserve at Disney World? _____103–132_____

Reading and Thinking

1. Check the sentence that best states the main idea of this story.
   ____ Meetings in Florida are fun.
   ____ Ben will travel to Disney World.
   _✓_ Disney World has special programs.

2. Write one thing that might change in your neighborhood if all the birds left.
   There would be more insects.
   (Answers may vary.)

3. Check the reason the author probably wrote this story.
   ____ to tell about wildlife
   _✓_ to tell about a nature preserve within an amusement park
   ____ to tell about energy

Write F before the sentences that are facts. Write O before the sentences that are opinions.

4. _F_ The nature preserve at Disney World covers hundreds of acres.
5. _O_ Everyone would like the nature program.
6. _F_ Binoculars can be used to watch birds more closely.
7. _O_ Bugs aren't good for anything.

Working with Words

Fill in each blank with the possessive form of the word in parentheses.

1. The _____preserves'_____ animals are fun to watch. (preserves)
2. Some _____trees'_____ leaves are food for the bugs. (trees)
3. _____Birds'_____ habits are studied at the nature preserve. (birds)

59

Knowing the Words

Write the words from the story that have the meanings below.

1. looked _____peered_____
   (Par. 5)
2. force of the earth _____gravity_____
   (Par. 10)
3. act of sending off _____launch_____
   (Par. 10)

A synonym is a word with the same or nearly the same meaning as another word. Circle each pair of synonyms.

4. (close—near) 7. (teacher—instructor)
5. part—whole 8. above—beneath
6. (space—area) 9. filled—empty

Match the word in the first column with its abbreviation.

10. _b_ Alabama a. Thurs.
11. _c_ Canada b. AL
12. _a_ Thursday c. CAN

Learning to Study

This is part of an application for Space Camp. Read the application form and answer the questions. Then fill out the form.

Name	Last	First	Middle
Address	Number	Street	
	City	State	Zip
Birth date	Day	Month	Year

1. What part of the name is written last?
   _____middle_____
2. Does the application ask for facts about the day you were born? _____yes_____
3. What two things are written on the first address line? _____number, street_____

Reading and Thinking

1. Number the events to show the order in which they happened.
   _5_ Ben was told about the moonship.
   _4_ Ben saw Apollo 16.
   _1_ Ben read about Space Camp.
   _2_ Ben got permission to go to Space Camp.
   _3_ Ben went to the new training center.

Circle the word that best completes each sentence.

2. The first few pages of my notebook kept ____ together when I turned them.
   spending (sticking) training
3. The group leader ____ the space suit so we could see how it looked.
   (modeled) traveled talked
4. Do you think Ben enjoyed the museum? Why or why not? _____
   (Answers will vary.)
5. If he could, do you think Ben would like to travel in space? Why or why not?
   _____
   (Answers will vary.)

Working with Words

Fill in each blank with the possessive form of the word in parentheses.

1. Ben thought the _____astronauts'_____ cabins were very small. (astronauts)
2. Both _____museums'_____ collections interest the tourists. (museums)
3. While he was gone, Ben read his _____classmates'_____ letters. (classmates)

61

Knowing the Words

Write the words from the story that have the meanings below.

1. condition of having no force of gravity _____weightlessness_____
   (Par. 1)
2. not clear _____blur_____
   (Par. 10)

Check the meaning of the homograph as it is used in the sentence.

3. We watched a TV program about space.
   ____ printed facts about a performance
   _✓_ a scheduled show
4. The girl had to rest after the long trip.
   _✓_ relax
   ____ what is left over

Learning to Study

Write the number of the encyclopedia volume that would have the most information for each topic. Remember that a person is listed by his or her last name.

Vol. 1 A–C	Vol. 2 D–F	Vol. 3 G–J	Vol. 4 K–M	Vol. 5 N–Q	Vol. 6 R–T	Vol. 7 U–Z

1. _3_ John Glenn 3. _6_ Sally Ride
2. _1_ astronauts 4. _5_ planets

Read the weather forecast below. Then answer the questions.

> Weather Forecast
> for the Los Angeles area
> —Cloudy and cooler Friday
> —Low temperature Friday around 50
> —Wind and rain Saturday
> —High temperature 65 Saturday

5. What day will be windy? _____Saturday_____
6. How cool will it be Friday? _____50_____
7. Will the sky be clear Saturday? _____No_____

Reading and Thinking

1. Check the sentence that best states the main idea of the story.
   _✓_ The campers learn about gravity.
   ____ The campers taste space food.
   ____ A spacecraft can go out of control.

2. Why did the seat in the frame spin in all directions? to help astronauts learn to steady a spacecraft that starts to tumble out of control

3. Why was it hard to work underwater?
   The tools floated around.
   (Answers may vary.)

4. Do you think Joy likes to try new things? Why or why not? _____
   (Answers will vary.)

Write C before the words that describe what the campers did. Write J before the words that describe what Jean did.

5. _C_ sat in a chair and felt weightless
6. _J_ tumbled inside a steel frame
7. _C_ worked in a pool with tools
8. _J_ gave out face masks
9. _J_ pointed to objects underwater
10. _J_ felt dizzy

Working with Words

Write a compound word using two words in each sentence.

1. A ball that you kick is a _____kickball_____.
2. A berry that is blue is a _____blueberry_____.
3. A storm of snow is a _____snowstorm_____.
4. A craft in outer space is a _____spacecraft_____.

63

Knowing the Words

Write the words from the story that have the meanings below.

1. a type of spacecraft _____shuttle_____
   (Par. 1)
2. knobs that turn _____dials_____
   (Par. 9)
3. expressed happiness about success of something _____congratulated_____
   (Par. 13)
4. something used to produce energy _____fuel_____
   (Par. 14)

Draw a line under the homophone that correctly completes each sentence.

5. Joy could ____ the loud noises.
   (here, hear)
6. We were at camp for five ____.
   (daze, days)
7. Idioms are groups of words that have special meanings. Write the idiom found in paragraph 3.
   ideas that were off the wall

Learning to Study

A library book can be listed in the card catalog or computer reference system by the author. Books are entered by the author's last name. Use the following information to answer the questions.

> CALL NO: 473.02
> AUTHOR: Kirk, Roberta
> MAIN TITLE: The Worlds of Space
> PUBLISHER: James Press, 1993

1. What is the author's name? _____Roberta Kirk_____
2. Under what name would this author be entered in a computer reference system or a card catalog? _____Kirk_____

Reading and Thinking

Circle the word that best completes each sentence.

1. A ____ of experts discussed the ideas and made a fair decision.
   control command (panel)
2. The captain took ____ of the ship.
   (charge) information practice

Write T before the sentences that are true. Write F before the sentences that are false.

3. _T_ Meg built and launched a rocket.
4. _F_ Ben helped to pilot the shuttle.
5. _T_ The crew taped Ben at Space Camp.
6. _F_ The flight had no problems.

7. Write a sentence from the story that tells you the campers at Mission Control were happy with the launch.
   The campers in Ben's group congratulated each other on the success of the launch.

8. In what way could space launches change in the future? _____
   (Answers will vary.)

Working with Words

Underline the word in each sentence that has a prefix. Then write the meaning of the underlined word in the blank.

1. The project was incomplete because the crew had not followed the rules.
   not complete
2. His inattention to time made him late.
   not paying attention

65

Knowing the Words

Write the words from the story that have the meanings below.

1. studies __research__ (Par. 3)
2. problems or subjects __issues__ (Par. 7)
3. take part in __participate__ (Par. 9)

A **synonym** is a word with the same or nearly the same meaning as another word. Write the pair of synonyms from each sentence.

4. The class listed their thoughts on the board, and the ideas were voted on.

__thoughts, ideas__

5. After we watched the movie, the artist showed us how the film was made.

__movie, film__

Learning to Study

1. Complete the following outline. Use paragraph 3 to complete Part I. Use paragraph 7 to complete Part II. (Answers may vary.)

I. Studying the chimps
 A. Worked to build trust
 B. __Learned that chimps use tools__
 C. __Learned that chimps eat meat__
II. Teaching through Roots and Shoots
 A. Teaches about the environment
 B. __Teaches about animal concerns__
 C. __Teaches about human concerns__

2. Number the words below in alphabetical order.

__5__ blame   __2__ believe
__4__ black   __3__ bike
__1__ badge   __6__ blank

Reading and Thinking

1. Check the sentence that best states the main idea of the story.
 ___ Jane Goodall works in Africa.
 ✓ Goodall studies and teaches.
 ___ Goodall started Roots and Shoots.

2. Number the events to show the order in which they happened.
 __4__ Goodall spoke about chimps.
 __1__ Jane Goodall went to Africa.
 __3__ Goodall learned chimps make tools.
 __5__ Goodall started Roots and Shoots.
 __2__ Goodall began studying chimps.

Write **F** before the sentences that are facts. Write **O** before the sentences that are opinions.

3. __F__ Chimps eat fruits, vegetables, and meat.
4. __F__ Goodall studied chimps in 1960.
5. __O__ Chimps are afraid of people.

6. What do you think Jane Goodall wants people to learn from Roots and Shoots?

(Answers will vary.)

Working with Words

Check the correct meaning of the underlined word.

1. Do not _misuse_ the new equipment.
 ✓ use badly
 ___ use before
 ___ use often

2. It is _impolite_ to interrupt the speaker.
 ___ very polite
 ✓ not polite
 ___ often polite

67

Knowing the Words

Write the words from the story that have the meanings below.

1. sport using thin swords __fencing__ (Par. 6)
2. trimmed with threads __fringed__ (Par. 7)
3. thin cloth for covering the face __veil__ (Par. 10)

Check the meaning of the underlined word in each sentence.

4. The actors walked through the crowd carrying a _trunk_ full of props.
 ___ the main part of something
 ✓ a large box with a lid

5. The musicians will _play_ for the dancers.
 ✓ make an instrument work
 ___ actions done for fun

Learning to Study

This chart tells about the events at the festival for two days. Use the chart to answer the questions.

EVENTS	SATURDAY	SUNDAY
Puppet show	2:00 and 4:00	2:00 and 4:00
Dancing	3:00 only	3:00 and 5:00
Fencing	1:00 and 3:00	1:00 only
Plays	2:00 and 4:00	2:00 and 4:00

1. What two events begin at the same time both days? __puppet show, plays__

2. On what day is dancing scheduled only one time? __Saturday__

3. What could you see at 4:00 on Sunday if you didn't want to see a play?

__puppet show__

Reading and Thinking

Write **T** before the sentences that are true. Write **F** before the sentences that are false.

1. __T__ Carmen gave Ling an idea for a show.
2. __T__ Carmen wore a hat.
3. __F__ Carmen rode on horseback.
4. __T__ The festival has a puppet show.

Write **E** before each group of words that describe events in an English village in the 1500s. Write **C** before each group of words that describe modern events.

5. __E__ knights riding horses
6. __C__ people driving cars
7. __E__ dancers on stilts
8. __E__ villagers using bows and arrows

9. Check the reason the author probably wrote this story.
 ✓ to tell about Carmen in a play
 ✓ to tell about a special festival
 ___ to tell about old-fashioned clothes

10. Do you think Carmen will share other ideas for the show? Why or why not?

(Answers will vary.)

Working with Words

Check the correct meaning of the underlined word.

1. He watched the play in _amazement_.
 ✓ the act of being amazed
 ___ not amazed
 ___ amazed before

2. She was _speechless_ during the show.
 ___ before speech
 ___ act of speech
 ✓ without speech

69

Knowing the Words

Write the words from the story that have the meanings below.

1. upset __disgusted__ (Par. 2)
2. leather straps used to hold something or someone __harness__ (Par. 9)
3. an explosive __dynamite__ (Par. 11)

Check the meaning of the homograph as it is used in each sentence.

4. Mom will _leave_ your presents with me.
 ✓ allow to remain behind
 ___ have permission to go

5. I _long_ to see my friends who have moved.
 ___ having greater length than usual
 ✓ wish for something

Learning to Study

1. Complete the following outline. Use paragraph 9 to complete Part I. Use paragraph 11 to complete Part II. (Answers may vary.)

I. Problems of getting to work
 A. __Workers rode horses or walked__
 B. __Workers climbed mountain for one-half hour__
II. Problems with cracked rock
 A. __Water might freeze__
 B. __Part of carving could break off__

Write these dictionary entry words in syllables to show where the words can be divided at the end of a line of writing.

2. scatter __scat / ter__
3. suppose __sup / pose__
4. surface __sur / face__

Reading and Thinking

1. Check the sentence that best states the main idea of the story.
 ✓ Gutzon Borglum is a famous artist.
 ___ Carving Mount Rushmore was difficult.
 ___ Carving an eagle is difficult.

Write **T** before the sentences that are true. Write **F** before the sentences that are false.

2. __T__ The heads of four presidents are carved into Mount Rushmore.
3. __F__ Mount Rushmore was finished in ten years.
4. __T__ Some workers walked to their jobs.

5. What might happen if the carving was not done in solid rock? __part of the carving might break off__

Circle the word that best completes each sentence.

6. The ___ of the box were counted.
 designs   (contents)   artists

7. The artist carved a ___ piece of wood.
 (solid)   tired   disgusted

Working with Words

Check the correct meaning of the underlined word.

1. The tape was _useless_ once it got tangled.
 ___ used
 ✓ without use
 ___ used before

2. Each child was given a _lovable_ puppy.
 ___ loved after
 ___ without love
 ✓ can be loved

71

Knowing the Words

Write the words from the story that have the meanings below.

1. eager to know __curious__ (Par. 4)
2. trying with great effort __struggling__ (Par. 5)
3. holds __grasps__ (Par. 9)

A **synonym** is a word with the same or nearly the same meaning as another word. Circle each pair of synonyms below.

4. (group—crowd)   7. natural—awkward
5. struggle—easy   8. (hurried—rushed)
6. friend—enemy   9. (smile—grin)

Learning to Study

Use the want ad below to answer the questions.

§ Paintings Wanted §
For Personal Collection
Paying top dollar
American artists only
Call M. Hill at 555-0011

1. Will M. Hill buy or sell paintings?
__buy__

2. Why does M. Hill want paintings?
__for a personal collection__

3. What kind of artists' paintings are wanted? __American__

Next to each artist's name below, write the encyclopedia letter you would use to find facts about the artist.

4. __R__ Frederic Remington
5. __C__ Mary Cassatt
6. __R__ Norman Rockwell
7. __O__ Georgia O'Keeffe

Reading and Thinking

1. What does Kim always carry?
__a backpack__

2. How does Daniel hold his paintbrush?
__with his toes__

3. Why is Daniel so good at using his feet to draw and paint? __He learned when he was growing up. (Answers may vary.)__

4. Do you think Daniel would be a good classmate? Why or why not? ___
__(Answers will vary.)__

5. Write the name of the character these words describe.
 polite   talented   determined
__Daniel__

Working with Words

Check the correct meaning of the underlined word.

1. If you are a _nonswimmer_ you must stay in the shallow end of the pool.
 ___ act of swimming
 ✓ not a swimmer
 ___ able to swim

2. He gave the teacher a _reasonable_ answer.
 ___ full of reasons
 ___ opposite of reason
 ✓ capable of having reason

3. The _homeless_ dog was wet and cold.
 ✓ without a home
 ___ before a home
 ___ not home

73

Knowing the Words

Write the words from the story that have the meanings below.

1. type of moveable home ___trailer___ (Par. 5)

2. certain condition ___situation___ (Par. 12)

Match the word in the first column with its abbreviation.

3. _b_ Mississippi **a.** IA
4. _c_ Minnesota **b.** MS
5. _a_ Iowa **c.** CN

6. An **idiom** is a group of words that has a special meaning. Write the idiom in paragraph 16.

___my idea was all wet___

Learning to Study

1. Complete the following outline. Use the facts in paragraph 5 to complete Part I. Use the facts in paragraphs 7–11 to complete Part II. (Answers may vary.)

I. Glen prepares for trip

A. _Made a raft_

B. _Started in Minneapolis_

C. _Arranged to meet crew in Iowa_

II. River accident

A. _Raft tipped_

B. _Crew fell into river_

C. _Motor sank_

2. Number the words below in alphabetical order.

_6_ drill   _1_ control
_3_ doubt   _5_ drift
_4_ dried   _2_ date

Reading and Thinking

1. Check the sentence that best states the main idea of the story.

___ Ling goes on a trip.

___ Ling helps plant trees.

_✓_ Ling describes taping a show.

Circle the word that correctly completes each sentence.

2. The girls played on the ___ in the pool at the apartment.

river (raft) motor

3. I can ___ to buy a present for my friend's birthday.

attach (afford) memory

Write **T** before the sentences that are true. Write **F** before the sentences that are false.

4. _F_ The trip started in Iowa.

5. _T_ The raft tipped over.

6. _F_ The crew's camera sank.

7. _T_ The townspeople helped Glen buy a new motor.

8. _T_ Glen planted trees along the way.

9. Write a summary for paragraph 13. Include the points given below.

Glen's friendliness   people's help

___Glen was friendly, so people liked him___

___and wanted to help buy a new motor.___

(Answers may vary.)

Working with Words

Write **S** if the possessive word is singular. Write **P** if the possessive word is plural.

1. _S_ pencil's   5. _P_ people's
2. _P_ trees'   6. _S_ camera's
3. _S_ raft's   7. _P_ jackets'
4. _P_ programs'   8. _S_ river's

75

Knowing the Words

Write the words from the story that have the meanings below.

1. made of copper and tin ___bronze___ (Par. 13)

2. something having a similar appearance ___likeness___ (Par. 13)

3. the acts of reaching a goal; successes ___achievements___ (Par. 13)

4. shown ___displayed___ (Par. 14)

Check the meaning of the underlined word in each sentence.

5. The diamond sparkled in the light.

___ infield in baseball

_✓_ jewel

6. The doctor said the patient was well.

___ willing to wait

_✓_ person treated by a doctor

7. The worker retired after twenty years.

___ went to bed

_✓_ stopped working

Learning to Study

Use the entry below to answer the questions.

bank /bangk/ n **1** place of business for handling money **2** the land around a river

1. Underline the sentence in which bank has the same meaning as the first definition.

Kate sat on the bank of the river.

The sports star put his savings in the bank.

2. Write a sentence that uses bank meaning "the land around a river."

___(Sentences will vary.)___

Reading and Thinking

Circle the word that best completes each sentence.

1. The ___ was made into a ring for Kay's birthday.

shoe (diamond) vest

2. The doctor had to ___ the child.

build sing (examine)

3. Check the reason the author probably wrote this story.

___ to tell the history of baseball

_✓_ to tell about the Chicago Cubs

___ to tell about Kate's sports hero

4. Write a sentence from the story that tells how anxious Kate is for baseball season to start.

___At the first sign of spring, you're out___

___on the diamond hitting balls and___

___catching grounders.___

5. Do you think Kate will continue to play baseball after her visit to New York? Why or why not?

___

___ (Answers will vary.)

Working with Words

Fill in each blank with the possessive form of the word in parentheses.

1. West View is the ___people's___ favorite park. (people)

2. The woman needed the ___sheep's___ wool to make the yarn. (sheep)

3. Brushing brightens the ___teeth's___ shine. (teeth)

77

Knowing the Words

Write the words from the story that have the meanings below.

1. a guard or keeper of a park ___ranger___ (Par. 4)

2. attacked and took something ___raided___ (Par. 11)

Underline the word with the correct meaning in each sentence below.

3. Kate ___ like to see the mudpot in the park. (would, wood)

4. Each rope on the tent had a ___ at the end. (knot, not)

A **synonym** is a word with the same or nearly the same meaning as another word. Write the pair of synonyms from each sentence.

5. He was on duty because no one else could do his job that day.

___duty, job___

6. The shops were filled with people who enjoyed looking through the stores.

___shops, stores___

Learning to Study

Write the letter you would look under to find facts in the encyclopedia to answer each of the questions below.

1. What does a ranger do? ___R___

2. How large is Yellowstone Park? ___Y___

3. What is Old Faithful? ___O___

4. What main topic could you look under to find facts in the encyclopedia that would answer questions 2 and 3?

___Yellowstone___ (Answers may vary.)

Reading and Thinking

1. Check the reason the author probably wrote this story.

___ to tell about a ranger

_✓_ to tell about bears at Yellowstone

___ to tell about camping in Yellowstone

Circle the word that best completes each sentence.

2. Ben's dad was ___ on Mr. Freeman to show them the park.

begging (counting) looking

3. We ___ to see her this week.

(plan) reach show

Write **Y** before the words that describe the bears in Yellowstone Park today. Write **B** before the words that describe the bears in Yellowstone Park before 1967.

4. _Y_ stay in back country

5. _Y_ more bears than ever before

6. _B_ raid garbage cans near hotels and shops

7. _B_ come up to cars of the visitors

8. Write a summary for paragraph 11. Include the points given below.

bears as a problem   plan for the bears

___The park started a plan to keep the___

___bears from being a problem to people.___

(Answers may vary.)

Working with Words

Fill in each blank with the possessive form of the word in parentheses.

1. The ___visitors'___ cars had green tags while in the park. (visitors)

2. The ___shop's___ owner liked working with the tourists. (shop)

79

Knowing the Words

Write the words from the story that have the meanings below.

1. leaks ___seeps___ (Par. 3)

2. a spring shooting steam into the air ___geyser___ (Par. 3)

3. saw for yourself ___witnessed___ (Par. 4)

4. solid material dug from the earth ___minerals___ (Par. 7)

A **synonym** is a word with the same or nearly the same meaning as another word. Write the words from the story that are synonyms for these words.

5. stone ___rock___ (Par. 3)

6. warmed ___heated___ (Par. 3)

7. climbing ___rising___ (Par. 6)

Learning to Study

Read the graph and answer the questions.

Tourists

Day 1
Day 2
Day 3
*0 2 4 6 8 10
*numbers are in thousands

1. What day had the largest number of tourists? ___Day 3___

2. What day had fewer than six thousand tourists? ___Day 2___

Syllables show where words can be divided at the end of a line of writing. Use a dictionary to write these words in syllables.

3. volcano ___vol / ca / no___

4. arrowheads ___ar / row / heads___

Reading and Thinking

1. Check the sentence that best states the main idea of this story.

___ Volcanoes can change the land.

___ Tourists come to enjoy the park.

_✓_ Yellowstone has interesting sights.

2. What is Old Faithful? ___a geyser___

3. What gives the mudpots their colors?

___minerals___

4. What did Native Americans make out of hard rock? ___arrowheads___

5. What caused the rock in Yellowstone to be yellow? ___lava from volcanoes turned the___

___rock yellow___

6. Why are Robyn and Eddie good guides for the Wilkins family? ___They enjoy___

___sharing what they know about the park.___

(Answers may vary.)

Working with Words

Write a compound word using two words in each sentence.

1. Balls thrown into baskets are

___basketballs___

2. An area of ground used as a place to camp is a ___campground___

3. A place under the surface of the ground is ___underground___

4. Wood used to burn in a fire is

___firewood___

81

Knowing the Words

Write the words from the story that have the meanings below.

1. walk a long distance ___hike___ (Par. 1)

2. given a duty ___stationed___ (Par. 7)

Underline the word with the correct meaning in each sentence below.

3. It took ___ hours to set up camp. (four, for)

4. Kate ___ strange sounds coming from the woods. (herd, heard)

5. Eddie was the ___ to tell the strange ghost story. (won, one)

6. Write the simile found in paragraph 10.

   ___a horse as black as night___

Learning to Study

This map shows Ft. Laramie and part of the Oregon Trail. Use the map to answer the questions below.

1. How many states are shown? ___5___

2. In what state is Ft. Laramie? ___Wyoming___

3. How many states on the map did this part of the Oregon Trail cross? ___4___

4. What two forts are in Idaho? ___Ft. Boise, Ft. Hall___

Reading and Thinking

Circle the word that best completes each sentence.

1. We ___ a tent in a clearing.
   followed   decided   (pitched)

2. The ranger has to ___ the wild bird.
   (catch)   vanish   rustle

3. Do you think Ben will tell the story of the Laramie Ghost to his friends? Why or why not? ___(Answers will vary.)___

4. Why didn't the lieutenant catch up to the woman on the black horse?
   ___She disappeared over a hill.___

Write **T** before the sentences that are true. Write **F** before the sentences that are false.

5. _F_ The woman left the fort this year.

6. _F_ Allison was the son of a settler.

7. _T_ The woman rode out of the fort.

8. Write a summary for paragraph 9. Include the points given below.
   Allison's try   rider's disappearance
   ___Allison tried to catch up with the___
   ___rider, but she and her horse disappeared.___
   ___(Answers may vary.)___

Working with Words

Write a compound word using two words in each sentence.

1. The beat from the hoof of a horse is a ___hoofbeat___.

2. A pack worn on your back is a ___backpack___.

83

Knowing the Words

Write the words from the story that have the meanings below.

1. a show of skill with horses and cattle ___rodeo___ (Par. 4)

2. trust ___confidence___ (Par. 12)

Check the meaning of the underlined word in each sentence.

3. Rose wanted to bowl on Thursday nights, but the league was closed.
   ___ a dish with high sides
   _✓_ play a game by rolling a ball

4. He turned right at the corner.
   ___ correct
   _✓_ a direction

Learning to Study

Read this recipe Ben might follow when he cooks. Then answer the questions.

Pancakes	
1 cup flour	1 cup milk
2 teaspoons baking powder	1 egg
2 tablespoons sugar	3 tablespoons butter (melted)
¼ teaspoon salt	

Mix flour, baking powder, sugar, and salt in medium bowl. Beat egg, add milk and butter, beat again. Pour into bowl with flour mixture and stir till lumpy. Pour 1/4 cup batter into hot pan for each pancake. Cook till bubbles form on top. Turn and cook 2 minutes longer.

1. Write the items that are mixed with the flour.
   ___baking powder, sugar, salt___

2. How much batter is needed for each pancake? ___1/4 cup___

3. What kind of butter is used? ___melted___

Reading and Thinking

Write **F** before the sentences that are facts. Write **O** before the sentences that are opinions.

1. _F_ Robots aren't bothered by heat.

2. _O_ Summer vacations are boring.

3. _F_ A rodeo is held in Houston.

4. _O_ Mammoth Cave is fun to visit.

5. _F_ People go snorkeling in Florida.

6. Check the sentence that best states the main idea of the story.
   _✓_ The family shares ideas for the new season of Ben's show.
   ___ The Wilkins family has a picnic.
   ___ The family plans a trip to Florida.

7. Why does Ben need ideas for the show?
   ___The show's first meeting is in two weeks.___

8. Does Ben trust himself? Why or why not? ___(Answers will vary.)___

Working with Words

Write a compound word using two words in each sentence.

1. Water that has salt in it is ___saltwater___

2. A book used for taking notes is a ___notebook___

3. A person who makes sales is a ___salesperson___

4. A cloth that covers a table is a ___tablecloth___

85

Checking Understanding

Test 1   These exercises are to be completed after reading the story on page 10.

1. The event takes place in ___Arlington National Cemetery___.

2. Check the reason the event is called the Changing of the Guard.
   ___ Both soldiers change directions.
   ___ The two soldiers are called guards.
   _✓_ One guard replaces another guard.

3. What does the officer do?
   ___inspects guard___

4. Underline two sentences that are true. (2)
   Tourists see the Changing of the Guard.
   The buried soldiers are unknown.
   The guards talk to each other.
   Tourists take part in the ceremony.

5. The soldier guarding the tomb is a part of an ___honor guard___.

6. Check the main idea of the story.
   ___ Touring Washington, D.C., is fun.
   ___ Honor guards are soldiers.
   _✓_ The Changing of the Guard is a special ceremony.

7. Check two actions both soldiers do during the ceremony (2)
   ___ change rifles   _✓_ tap heels
   _✓_ pace   ___ salute

8. What does an honor guard need to be able to do?
   _✓_ march to music
   _✓_ know the cemetery history
   ___ name the soldiers buried in the Tomb of the Unknowns

Number of Words Read per Minute [ ]
Test Score (Possible Score–10) [ ]

Test 2   These exercises are to be completed after reading the story on page 32.

1. Where did Laurie live when she became interested in lighthouses?
   ___Maine___

2. Check what was used to build the first Boston Light.
   ___ steel   _✓_ wood   ___ bricks

3. Check the two things that often caused lighthouses to be destroyed. (2)
   _✓_ fire   _✓_ storms   ___ rocks

4. What do modern lighthouses look like?
   ___radio towers___

5. What now runs some modern lighthouses? ___computers___

6. Why is steel used to build new lighthouses? ___It is sturdier and it won't burn. (Answers may vary.)___

7. Who rescued sailors? ___lighthouse keepers___

8. Check two sentences that are true. (2)
   _✓_ Lighthouses have changed.
   _✓_ Boston Light is on an island.
   ___ Today, lighthouses use fire for light.
   ___ Lighthouses always help ships.

Number of Words Read per Minute [ ]
Test Score (Possible Score–10) [ ]

86

Checking Understanding

Test 3   These exercises are to be completed after reading the story on page 52.

1. Mount St. Helens is in what state?
   ___Washington___

2. Check the sentence that is true.
   _✓_ The volcano in Mount St. Helens exploded in 1980.
   ___ Lava flowed out of Mount St. Helens.
   ___ Nothing can live on Mount St. Helens.

3. Why does Carmen's brother know so much about volcanoes and earthquakes?
   ___He is a scientist. (Answers may vary.)___

4. Why was Joe at Mount St. Helen's when it exploded? ___He was studying earthquakes.___

5. What caused the ice on the mountain to melt? ___heat from the explosion___

6. The fish in the nearest river were destroyed because ___the water was 90 degrees___

7. Check three signs of life on the mountain. (3)
   _✓_ flowers   ___ melted rock
   ___ lava   _✓_ ferns
   ___ ash   _✓_ deer tracks

8. Ash fell in towns as far away as ___five hundred miles___

Number of Words Read per Minute [ ]
Test Score (Possible Score–10) [ ]

Test 4   These exercises are to be completed after reading the story on page 78.

1. Check the main idea of the story.
   ___ camping accidents
   ___ trip to Wyoming
   _✓_ bears in a national park

2. Mr. Freeman knows about Yellowstone Park because ___he is a park ranger___.

3. Write the three actions taken to protect tourists against the bears. (3)
   ___closed the garbage areas, tourists___
   ___didn't feed bears, bears were caught___
   ___and taken to other parts of the park___

4. How long did it take to rid the tourist areas of bears? ___10 years___

5. Why were bears found around the hotels? ___They were eating garbage from the cans. (Answers may vary.)___

6. Check one reason fences weren't used to control the bears.
   ___ harmful to bears
   _✓_ size of park
   ___ materials not available

7. Why were bears kept in the woods? ___so people wouldn't be hurt by the bears___

8. Check the sentence that is true.
   _✓_ Yellowstone has more bears now than ever.
   ___ Bears have left Yellowstone Park.
   ___ All park hotels are closed.

Test Score (Possible Score–10) [ ]

87

NOTES

SPECTRUM

Brought to you by McGraw-Hill, the premier educational publisher for grades PreK–12.
All our workbooks meet school curriculum guidelines and correspond to
The McGraw-Hill Companies' classroom textbooks.

LANGUAGE ARTS

Grades 3–6 • 160 full-color pages
Size: 8.375" x 10.875" • Paperback

Encourages creativity and builds confidence by making writing fun! Sixty four-part lessons strengthen writing skills by focusing on parts of speech, word usage, sentence structure, punctuation, and proofreading. This series is based on the highly respected SRA/McGraw-Hill language arts series. Answer key included.

MATH

Grades K–8 • Over 150 pages
Size: 8.375" x 10.875" • Paperback

Features easy-to-follow instructions that give students a clear path to success. This series includes comprehensive coverage of the basic skills, helping children master math fundamentals. Answer key included.

PHONICS/WORD STUDY

Grades K–6 • Over 200 pages
Size: 8.375" x 10.875" • Paperback

Provides everything children need to build multiple skills in language arts. This series focuses on phonics, structural analysis, and dictionary skills, and offers creative ideas for using phonics and word study skills in language areas. Answer key included.

READING

Grades K–6 • Over 150 full-color pages
Size: 8.375" x 10.875" • Paperback

This full-color series creates an enjoyable reading environment, even for below-average readers. Each book contains captivating content, colorful characters, and compelling illustrations, so children are eager to find out what happens next. Answer key included.

TITLE	ISBN	PRICE
LANGUAGE ARTS		
Gr. 3	1-57768-483-4	$8.95
Gr. 4	1-57768-484-2	$8.95
Gr. 5	1-57768-485-0	$8.95
Gr. 6	1-57768-486-9	$8.95
MATH		
Gr. K	1-57768-400-1	$8.95
Gr. 1	1-57768-401-X	$8.95
Gr. 2	1-57768-402-8	$8.95
Gr. 3	1-57768-403-6	$8.95
Gr. 4	1-57768-404-4	$8.95
Gr. 5	1-57768-405-2	$8.95
Gr. 6	1-57768-406-0	$8.95
Gr. 7	1-57768-407-9	$8.95
Gr. 8	1-57768-408-7	$8.95
PHONICS (Grades K–3)/WORD STUDY and PHONICS (Grades 4–6)		
Gr. K	1-57768-450-8	$8.95
Gr. 1	1-57768-451-6	$8.95
Gr. 2	1-57768-452-4	$8.95
Gr. 3	1-57768-453-2	$8.95
Gr. 4	1-57768-454-0	$8.95
Gr. 5	1-57768-455-9	$8.95
Gr. 6	1-57768-456-7	$8.95
READING		
Gr. K	1-57768-460-5	$8.95
Gr. 1	1-57768-461-3	$8.95
Gr. 2	1-57768-462-1	$8.95
Gr. 3	1-57768-463-X	$8.95
Gr. 4	1-57768-464-8	$8.95
Gr. 5	1-57768-465-6	$8.95
Gr. 6	1-57768-466-4	$8.95

Prices subject to change without notice.

SPELLING

Grades 3–6 • 160 full-color pages
Size: 8.375" x 10.875" • Paperback

This full-color series links spelling to reading and writing, and increases skills in words and meanings, consonant and vowel spellings, and proofreading practice. Speller dictionary and answer key included.

VOCABULARY

Grades 3–6 • 160 full-color pages
Size: 8.375" x 10.875" • Paperback

An essential building block for writing and reading proficiency, this series extends vocabulary knowledge through grade-appropriate instruction and activities. Synonyms, antonyms, homophones, word families, and word forms are among the key concepts explored. Instruction is based on language arts and reading standards, offering a solid foundation for language arts, spelling, and reading comprehension. The series features a proficiency test practice section for standards-aligned assessment. Answer key included.

WRITING

Grades 3–6 • 160 full-color pages
Size: 8.375" x 10.875" • Paperback

Lessons focus on creative and expository writing using clearly stated objectives and pre-writing exercises. Eight essential reading skills are applied. Activities include main idea, sequence, comparison, detail, fact and opinion, cause and effect, making a point, and point of view. Each book includes a Writer's Handbook that offers writing tips. Answer key included.

TEST PREP

Grades 1–8 • 160 full-color pages
Size: 8.375" x 10.875" • Paperback

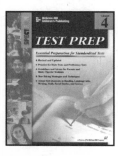

This series teaches the skills, strategies, and techniques necessary for students to succeed on any standardized test. Each book contains guidelines and advice for parents along with study tips for students. Grades 1 and 2 cover Reading, Language Arts, Writing, and Math. Grades 3 through 8 cover Reading, Language Arts, Writing, Math, Social Studies, and Science.

FLASH CARDS

Card size: 3.0625" x 4.5625"

Flash cards provide children with one of the most effective ways to drill and practice fundamentals. The cards have large type, making it easy for young learners to read them. Each pack contains 50 flash cards, including a parent instruction card that offers suggestions for fun, creative activities and games that reinforce children's skills development.

TITLE	ISBN	PRICE
SPELLING		
Gr. 3	1-57768-493-1	$8.95
Gr. 4	1-57768-494-X	$8.95
Gr. 5	1-57768-495-8	$8.95
Gr. 6	1-57768-496-6	$8.95
VOCABULARY		
Gr. 3	1-57768-793-0	$8.95
Gr. 4	1-57768-794-9	$8.95
Gr. 5	1-57768-795-7	$8.95
Gr. 6	1-57768-796-5	$8.95
WRITING		
Gr. 3	1-57768-913-5	$8.95
Gr. 4	1-57768-914-3	$8.95
Gr. 5	1-57768-915-1	$8.95
Gr. 6	1-57768-916-X	$8.95
TEST PREP		
Gr. 1–2	1-57768-662-4	$9.95
Gr. 3	1-57768-663-2	$9.95
Gr. 4	1-57768-664-0	$9.95
Gr. 5	1-57768-665-9	$9.95
Gr. 6	1-57768-666-7	$9.95
Gr. 7	1-57768-667-5	$9.95
Gr. 8	1-57768-668-3	$9.95
FLASH CARDS		
Addition	1-57768-167-3	$2.99
Alphabet	1-57768-151-7	$2.99
Division	1-57768-158-4	$2.99
Money	1-57768-150-9	$2.99
Multiplication	1-57768-157-6	$2.99
Numbers	1-57768-127-4	$2.99
Phonics	1-57768-152-5	$2.99
Sight Words	1-57768-160-6	$2.99
Subtraction	1-57768-168-1	$2.99
Telling Time	1-57768-138-X	$2.99

Prices subject to change without notice.

SPECTRUM

SPECTRUM WORKBOOKS
ILLUSTRATED BY MERCER MAYER!

Grades K–2 • 128–160 full-color pages • Size: 8.375" x 10.875" • Paperback

McGraw-Hill, the premier educational publisher for grades PreK–12, and acclaimed children's author and illustrator, Mercer Mayer, are the proud creators of this workbook line featuring the lovable Little Critter. Like other Spectrum titles, the length, breadth, and depth of the activities in these workbooks enable children to learn a variety of skills about a single subject.

- Mercer Mayer's Little Critter family of characters has sold over 50 million books. These wholesome characters and stories appeal to both parents and teachers.
- Each full-color workbook is based on highly respected McGraw-Hill Companies' textbooks.
- All exercises feature easy-to-follow instructions.
- An answer key is included in each workbook.

TITLE	ISBN	PRICE
LANGUAGE ARTS		
Grade K	1-57768-840-6	$8.95
Grade 1	1-57768-841-4	$8.95
Grade 2	1-57768-842-2	$8.95
MATH		
Grade K	1-57768-800-7	$8.95
Grade 1	1-57768-801-5	$8.95
Grade 2	1-57768-802-3	$8.95
PHONICS		
Grade K	1-57768-820-1	$8.95
Grade 1	1-57768-821-X	$8.95
Grade 2	1-57768-822-8	$8.95
READING		
Grade K	1-57768-810-4	$8.95
Grade 1	1-57768-811-2	$8.95
Grade 2	1-57768-812-0	$8.95
SPELLING		
Grade K	1-57768-830-9	$8.95
Grade 1	1-57768-831-7	$8.95
Grade 2	1-57768-832-5	$8.95
WRITING		
Grade K	1-57768-850-3	$8.95
Grade 1	1-57768-851-1	$8.95
Grade 2	1-57768-852-X	$8.95

Prices subject to change without notice.

Wholesome, well-known characters plus proven school curriculum equals learning success!

Coming in June 2003!

TITLE	ISBN	PRICE
PRESCHOOL		
Basic Concepts	1-57768-509-1	$8.95
Letters and Sounds	1-57768-539-3	$8.95
Numbers and Counting	1-57768-519-9	$8.95
Reading Readiness	1-57768-529-6	$8.95
Beginning Math	1-57768-579-2	$8.95
Beginning Phonics	1-57768-589-X	$8.95
Beginning Reading	1-57768-599-7	$8.95
Beginning Writing	1-57768-549-0	$8.95

Prices subject to change without notice.